BRUISED
BUT NOT BROKEN

Edited by Linda Ellis Eastman

Professional Woman Publishing
Prospect, Kentucky

BRUISED BUT NOT BROKEN
Copyright © 2010 by Linda Ellis Eastman

Published by:
Professional Woman Publishing
Post Office Box 333
Prospect, KY 40059
(502) 228-0906
www.pwnbooks.com

Please contact the publisher for quantity discounts.

ISBN 13: 978-0-9845827-2-3
ISBN 10: 098458272X

Library of Congress Cataloging-In-Publication Data

Cover Design and Typography by:
Sential Design, LLC — www.sentialdesign.com
Photo credits: Yuri Arcurs @ Dreamstime.com

Printed in the United States of America

Dedicated to Ivee Jo Roach who has weathered so many life storms and not only survived but flourished. Her kindness, warm heart and gentle spirit are a blessing to us all.

TABLE OF CONTENTS

TABLE OF CONTENTS
-CONTINUED-

TABLE OF CONTENTS
-CONTINUED-

ABOUT THE AUTHOR

LINDA ELLIS EASTMAN

Linda Ellis Eastman is President and CEO of The Professional Woman Network (PWN), an International Training and Consulting Organization on Women's Issues. She has designed seminars which have been presented in China, the former Soviet Union, South Africa, the Phillipines, and attended by individuals in the United States from such firms as McDonalds, USA Today, Siemens-Westinghouse, the Pentagon, the Department of Defense, and the United States Department of Education.

An expert on women's issues, Ms. Eastman has certified and trained over three thousand women to start consulting/seminar businesses originating from such countries as Pakistan, the Ukraine, Antigua, Canada, Mexico, Zimbabwe, Nigeria, Bermuda, Jamaica, Costa Rica, England, South Africa, Malaysia, and Kenya. Founded in 1982 by Linda Ellis Eastman, The Professional Woman Network is committed to educating women on a global basis regarding, self-esteem, confidence building, stress management, and emotional, mental, spiritual and physical wellness.

Ms. Eastman has been featured in USA Today and listed in Who's Who of American Women, as well as Who's Who of International Leaders. In addition to women's issues, Ms. Eastman speaks internationally regarding the importance of human respect as it relates to race, color, culture, age, and gender. She will be facilitating an international conference where speakers and participants from many nations will be able to discuss issues that are unique to women on a global basis.

Linda Ellis Eastman is also founder of The Professional Woman Speakers Bureau and The Professional Woman Coaching Institute. Ms. Eastman has dedicated her businesses to increasing the self-esteem and personal dignity of women and youth around the world.

Contact:
The Professional Woman Network
P.O. Box 333
Prospect, KY 40059
(502) 566-9900
lindaeastman@prodigy.net
www.pwnbooks.com
www.protrain.net

INTRODUCTION

Linda Ellis Eastman

Many women are victims of domestic abuse and young girls are increasingly subjected to sexual molestation on a daily basis, often by a family member. For these individuals there can be a difficult journey toward self-acceptance and positive self-esteem for they carry the burden of secrecy and shame.

If you or any family member has ever been to the 'bottom of the well' because of financial debt, toxic relationships, abuse, generational curses, or shame-based memories, this book is for you.

The authors have designed chapters which will help you to rebuild your life one step at a time. Very simply stated, they will guide you in starting over. Every woman deserves a second chance in life and no matter your past, it is time to face the future as a *victor* rather than a *victim*. The chapters will help you step out of toxic relationships, avoid abuse, and start living a joyous life.

You may have been bruised in life but no one can break your spirit. You will never be broken. May this book provide the ways to create the life of your dreams and forgive those who have harmed you but also create a life filled with healthy people who truly support and love you.

BRUISED
BUT NOT BROKEN

ABOUT THE AUTHOR

CHERYL WATKINS-KNOWLES

Cheryl.Knowles@aabpw.com

Cheryl Watkins-Knowles honors God and puts Him first in her life. She is a wife, mother and grandmother. She is the owner of American Association of Business and Professional Women (AABPW). AABPW's mission is to endow women with a sense of self, health and wealth; to be an organization of accomplished women where they work to improve themselves and other like minded women. A place to share ideas, interact in various professions while improving the network of business and professional women internationally. Cheryl sought a degree in Psychology and obtained a B.A. from Belford. Her civic duties include serving on the various Boards for community initiatives to include the Sickle Cell Circle of Hope Council. This council offers continued education to children and parents about the disease as well as provides fun opportunities like picnics, bowling and Residential camp while offering a physician on site for potential pain crisis events. She also has an advisory role for the local Chamber of Commerce on Women's business issues. She has spoken at national conferences, Church Organizations on topics such as supplier diversity inclusion and its importance to the community, Living a Thankful life and other issues related to the emotional health and healing of women from an economic, social and gender standpoint.

In her professional life she has held various positions from Manager to Director. She has consulted for several firms while developing best practice in the field of diversity, purchasing, supply chain and logistics. Her goal is to use metaphors for greater understanding. She has found that the use of figurative language, best teaches woman that they have the ability to learn and access the necessary life skills for the creation of a life of their own design.

She is family centered and her mentors are her grandfathers, the late Emit Watkins and Jesse Sparks Sr. as well as her father the late Lewis E. Watkins Sr. These men taught her the importance of Christianity, family values, responsibility, integrity, ethics and morals.

Join the American Association of Business and Professional Women and become the woman of your vision.

Cheryl does seminars, workshops, and keynotes on topics such as, leadership, personal and professional development, diversity, and business to business relationships. Cheryl is a certified professional coach and can be found at the Professional Woman Speakers Bureau, www.protrain.net.

Contact:
www.aabpw.com

ONE

LIVING A THANKFUL LIFE

By Cheryl Watkins-Knowles

To live thankfully you must have the appropriate cosmetics in your "make-up bag", as this will allow you to have the ability to choose the proper item to enhance yourself in any given situation. Think about applying make-up. There is a cosmetic product made to conquer every beauty challenge you may face. Likewise, the right life skill can help enhance your ability to overcome or tolerate any obstacle or challenge that you may experience in life. Without the proper skill or application of it, we can flounder and continue life in a daze or haze. This hazy existence leads to a life where we are not sure of the future, and often uncertain of our interpretation of the past. You may feel as if you are held hostage in an earlier period in life where there is no thankfulness.

To live a thankful life you must realize that there are a range of thoughts and emotions that you will experience in any given situation, and those thoughts and emotions are valid and justified based on your values and family background. However, to remain at any one of the stages without moving to the next, in a healthy amount of time, could be detrimental. So, let's talk about being thankful in spite of events that could steal your happiness. What products do you need in the "cosmetics bag" to enhance your life?

One tool you need in the cosmetic case is "**love**", which is the basis for a thankful life, and is similar to always carrying "foundation" in your make-up bag, because it creates a canvas for your other skills. Not the ordinary word we know of as Love. Not the love of a brother or the love of a sister. Not even the love of a husband or a wife. The love in which I am speaking of is "Agape Love", also known as God's love. This type of love is of and from God. I want you to take a moment and think of this type of love. Everything God does for us is from His love, and is a demonstration of it. The love God has for us is so wonderful that it is sometimes difficult to understand or imagine. We do nothing to warrant Agape Love. All we do is live. By living, we are given this love that we may know the importance of existence. Just as we are flawed, so are other individuals, and we must learn to express love without judgment or expectations. Take this moment and ask God to receive salvation, and ask the Lord to bring individuals into your space that will demonstrate Agape love. Once you have used all of your senses to experience God's blessing, and witnessed to others in your life, providing acceptance for you with genuine warmth and affection, you will be able to give Agape love to yourself and others. Take the time and patience to love yourself and others unconditionally. Every morning look into the mirror and repeat the affirmation audibly to yourself and say, "I love you" and "God loves you." Practice doing nice things for people. Do kind deeds when you are happy with them, as well as when you are not. Make a conscious decision to love yourself and others unconditionally.

Positive Thought

Now that you have decided to live in love, what other "beauty product" do you need in the "make-up bag"? Always include **"concealer"**, which blends the imperfections like "**Positive Thought**" does by turning negatives into positives. Have positive thoughts throughout the day. Did you know that positive and negative thoughts cannot exist in the mind at the same time? It's like good and evil cannot exist in the same location. If you do not believe me, try it. I want you to think of a bad experience; now think of a good one. What happened? The bad experience was moved out by the good experience, right? You have just taught yourself the importance of controlling your thoughts. When you control your thoughts, you realize who manages your mind. You do, and you do so by controlling your thoughts. This will help you learn to control your emotions! Just as we exercise our bodies to become fit, we also must work out our mind to develop the skill of positive thinking. Think happy thoughts and surround yourself with a sphere of influence that will encourage and aid you in maintaining a positive mind set. Choose to be around optimistic people. Proverb 23:7 says, *"For as he thinketh in his heart, so is he..."* So as a woman thinks, so is she. A portion of the law of energy says, whatever thoughts we continue to have will eventually manifest. So if you yearn for better results, change the way you think. Do not allow unconstructive thoughts to have an influence over your life. If you say to yourself, "my life will never change," then go ahead and settle for the life you currently have, because that is what you will get – a life that will never change. Make a decision to reflect on good things. Choose to love and think optimistically.

Goal Setting

Just as we would not forget to include mascara, do not leave home and forget to add "**Goal Setting**" to your make-up bag. Visualize yourself achieving a goal. Observe the emotion, physical sensations, and thoughts that accompany this image regarding how you will feel when you achieve the aspiration. Enjoy the moment, and do one thing every day to help you reach the objective. When the naysayers appear and attempt to harm or take away your dream, smile and kindly say, "Thank you for your opinion, but I don't agree," and think on achieving the goal. In those moments, push the negative thoughts that accompany their words out of your mind, and remember the feelings and sensations associated with the achievement of the desired outcome. Keep in mind that a negative and positive thought cannot exist at the same time. You may choose to think on bad things, or think on good things. Make the choice. Change your thoughts to see the world through rose colored glasses, and when the glasses turn to grey, press on and seek the affirmative. Always look for the rainbow. If you look you will find it, or knock and the door will open. If you wake and say to yourself, "My life is changing for the better every day," it will. Goals have a way of forcing us to focus on accomplishments. When you pursue your goal, only accept the outside influences that help to stimulate the creativity in you so that you can become a more positive person.

Positive People

Positive people pose various proficiencies. Like lip liner, these people fill uneven areas of your life, so throw it in the make-up bag. Think of a person you like being around. Someone you feel naturally drawn to because of their wonderful attitude. You know the ones. They are admired by many. They always have a kind word. They find the silver lining in every experience. Some people are born with these skills, and some are developed. Become the person with those skills. Put the right make-up in the bag to address the job at hand. Daily, state to yourself and others a positive affirmation about what you want out of life. When faced with not being able to achieve a desired result, be reminded that the operative word in this sentence is "not", and therefore has a negative connotation. Say to yourself, "I can achieve my life's ambition, and all the essential items in the universe will make themselves available to me because I am loved. God's Agape Love provides acceptance for me today, without a need to be someone different. I have all that I need to accomplish my goal through God's grace, favor, and protection, which covers me and allows for the rejection of negativity. I set goals and I surround myself with positive people. I am thankful and so is my inner circle."

Have you ever been told birds of a feather flock together? In 1545, William Turner coined this phrase, and we can still see it in practice today. The people you are around have an effect on how you feel. When surrounded by thankful people, you may find yourself looking at situations differently. Do not surround yourself with toxic people at work, or in social settings. Psychologist and author Dr. Lillian Glass describes these individuals as those who you allow to make you feel angry, confused, and irritated. These individuals are seriously damaging to your psychological and physical health. When faced with toxic people, politely excuse yourself from their presence, or block their influence by constantly affirming, encouraging, and validating yourself mentally. When you are around negative people for long periods of time, they tend to drain you of your vigor, and suck away your positive energy. Most people who have encountered these situations say, "I am so thankful I can choose to remove myself from negative people." Decide to establish a network of positive people. Make a list of those persons, and promise to communicate with them often. These people want your success and dreams to come true. This group of positive people accepts you where you are and support and gently push you in the direction that you dream to attain.

Affirmations

It is as important to include a set of previously established **"Affirmations"** in your make-up case, as it is to include a variety of lipsticks. Make these scripts part of your daily life. Post notes around your office, cubicle, desk, forklift, bathroom mirror, or anywhere you can quickly glance to read them. Read them daily and often. Expect your life to transform and be resolved with the opportunities that will appear. You were placed on this earth for great things, and God has plans for you. An affirmation to that statement might be, "I am thankful that God has great plans for me." These declarations help us shatter restraining thoughts or values so we are able to fashion new ones. Assume for a moment you strongly dislike your job. As you think this thought daily, you will always dislike your job. To live thankfully, you might say, "I am thankful I have the ability to search for new employment," or "I'm thankful to have a job." As you encounter others with the lifestyle that you desire, remember to continue using the aforementioned "products" in your "make-up bag", so that you do not project negative energy without the conscious realization.

Appreciation

Many would say that blush is important to complete any beauty look, and so is the inclusion of **"Appreciation"** in your bag. Always keep in mind that being appreciative for the success of others is paramount to living a thankful lifestyle. Look into your core, remove any jealously, envy, and strife by acknowledging that it exists, and decide to counteract those feelings by making statements to the contrary of those emotions. If a friend or an acquaintance is promoted, obtains a lovely house, gets a new car, is accepted into a sorority, or experiences any great event in their life, find delight in their fortune. It is easy to do so by replacing the harmful thought with a constructive one. Send the person a congratulatory card. Act on the positive feeling that you would have if you achieved their goal. When you can find joy in the blessings others receive, you will also be blessed.

Including **"Faith"** in your skill set is similar to including pressed powder in your make-up bag. It is a powerful tool that sets everything in place. It is written in Matthew 17:20, *"…I tell you the truth, if you have faith as small as a mustard seed, you can say to this mountain, 'Move from here to there' and it will move. Nothing will be impossible for you."* If we believe a mountain can be moved, all we need to do is say it and it will move. Be grateful that you can move mountains. Christians believe that *"…faith is the assurance of things hoped for, a conviction of things not seen."* (Hebrews 11:1). So if I want to live a thankful and grateful life, all I need to do is have the faith. Martin Luther King said, "Faith is taking the first step, even if you don't see the staircase." When you confidently believe in a person or concept, you demonstrate faith. It's a belief in a life that you can design which is worth living, and not just existing in day to day. It requires trust and reliance on yourself. Be mindful that subjecting your thoughts to the harmful actions that are imposed on victims by perpetrators may cause you to find yourself slipping into pessimism, forgetting to have faith. Therefore, selectively choose what you observe; and if you experience dire emotions, pick up faith, open the Good Book, say your affirmations having trust in the future. One such affirmation is, *"Today is the day the Lord has made, and I will rejoice and be glad in it."*

Now is the time for the **"Eyeliner"** to be placed in the bag. It is like picking up "**forgiveness**" and deciding to enhance the contours of the "eye" and life. By walking in forgiveness, you are opening the doors to a thankful life. Holding onto anger, vengeance, resentment, hate, and righteousness alters your soul. Forgiveness is not saying the act against you was warranted, but it is saying that for me to become who I am, this event had to occur. Looking through this perspective allows you to release negative emotions that strip you of happiness. When someone harms you, you go through a process of emotions. It is normal to ask ourselves, "Why did this happen to me?" We may even see it as emotionally, physically, or financially draining. If these circumstances cause us to suffer, how does one live a thankful life and forgive? We sometimes ask how we can feel grateful or satisfied when the future holds changes that are not always what we would select for ourselves. Be reminded that forgiveness cleans your heart.

Assume with me that your soul, which I am defining as your mind, will, and emotions, seeks to be blissful. Assume the state of blissfulness is a brilliant diamond. Holding on to unconstructive feelings is equal to a diamond with flaws. Once you actually forgive the person, you may find you have compassion for the person. That's okay because it is only the power of being thankful that alters your thoughts. Remember, when you don't forgive you hold on to the role of a victim. A victim passes the power of control to the person that committed the offense. Take back the control of your life, and decide to forgive. Give the gift of forgiveness to anyone that has wronged you, and re-establish your power so that you may have what you truly desire as a life worth living.

Giving

The act of **"Giving"** is a skill which is akin to including **"eye shadow"** in your make-up bag. It adds depth and dimension to your life. Instant satisfaction can be attained through conferring blessings that may make someone's life better. Think of a time when you gave gifts to a friend or loved one. When they opened the box, did you smile? Why? Was it because you received joy in giving joy? Maybe you felt angry because you didn't have the money or the time to give, but you did so out of responsibility or obligation. What I will ask you is this – did the person receiving the gift feel happiness? I'm sure the response is "yes." Therefore, in giving through obligation or responsibility you provided enjoyment. Bask in their delight, and feel their emotions as your own. To practice giving, do something kind for someone. When you arrive at an elevator before another person, ask them to go first. When in line at the grocery store, offer to let the person behind you go first. Buy an older couple or a single parent movie tickets, popcorn and sodas. Once you practice giving small things, then you can step it up a notch and practice giving more of your time or meeting the needs of others. Give time to a friend. Share the "make-up products" in the "make-up bag" with others. The next time you open your purse and catch a glimpse of your cosmetic bag, smile and share a skill that will help others cope with the daily hassles of life.

Controlling Negative Emotions

The last "product" to apply is **"Bronzer"**. It naturally blends together to give your skin a golden glow. This blending of skills can be accomplished by **"Controlling Negative Emotions"**. This one can be difficult, but can be accomplished. If a fire touches your skin, you burn, and most likely will feel pain and cry out. If you are hit with a thrown object, again you feel pain and cry out. If someone calls you ugly names, you will feel hurt. If someone says you are fat, you may feel sad and angry. My point here is negative things happen, but it is how we react to them that determine our soul's success. When you were small, you may have been taught to say, "Sticks and stones may break my bones but words will never harm me." How could we have known the wisdom that came from the idioms our parents taught? They were teaching us to deflect negativity. My dad would say, "Let those words bounce off you baby, they can only harm you if you allow them inside." I added to that, and told my daughter, "…and when you say it, put your hand on your hip, point your finger at them and say it in a sassy tone." The added actions of the body were a form of empowerment to reject the negativity and harm someone would wish upon her. Always look at your existence as if the glass were full, even if it appears empty. Bob Murphy, R.N., Esq., says, "What we permit, we promote." Therefore, do not allow anyone to steal away your joy and happiness. That includes you. The process to accomplish this task begins with you removing yourself from negative people, thoughts, and feelings. Do not allow them to fill your being with unconstructiveness. We then must replace negative people, thoughts, and emotions with their counter – positivity. If you are unable to eliminate sources of pessimistic energy from your life, you must block the negativity by creating a psychological chasm between yourself and others, which will serve as a container for the pessimism and separate you from becoming the receptacle for it while around those situations. Energetically reject negative thoughts, set goals, and affirm your dreams while being happy for the success of others.

You are at a fork in the road. You may want to remain in the past because it is more comfortable. Ask yourself, is this contented location where I want to be? Do I find happiness where I am currently? If the response is "no", then I suggest you pick up the *Thankful Life Make-Up Bag*. Your outlook on your life will improve significantly if you apply at least one of the tools. What do you have to lose? Changing the way a person views their life can take months or even years with psychological help. I suggest that you use these tools as a catalyst to achieve a better life.

Express gratitude in the face of adversity, and decide to be thankful. Wake in the morning and say "Thank You" to God. Recognize what you do have in the midst of hard times. Live in the moment and not in the past. Look at the blessings of others and be happy for their success. What I am asking you to do is to change your paradigm, or the way you think. I can't explain why bad things happen, but I can tell you any event that occurs in your life will help you to enrich your life. Look back on some small negative experience that occurred, however at the end of the day, a positive came from it. You must choose to be willing to respond to the life you have been given with thankfulness. To be willing, you must be aware of your mental state and react with a purposeful mind. When you accept the tools offered, you will act in a way to help yourself develop a purposeful mind. Focus on the effectiveness of the skill set developed here instead of the outcome achieved when the tools are used, because you only have control of yourself in life and not the outcomes.

Acceptance is a choice. Changing the mind to choose different thoughts is a form of acceptance. If your non-thankful life is going north, then a thankful life must head south. It's choosing to do a 180-degree turn, and making a commitment to use the "products" in the "make-up bag" in any given circumstance. It is quite okay if you sometimes forget to use the tools. In reality, it is about getting back on the horse after being thrown off. These are skills you must practice again, again and again. If you fall off the horse, get right back on and refocus. You will find that each time you apply a "make-up look," the "products" will become easier and easier to use.

You have the power to change! Once you put all of the tools together, you get a great "cosmetic bag", which can help create a better quality of life. With this new make-up bag, you will experience a life where you live with a sense of joy and thankfulness. Although, when experiencing the vast changes that come into your life, especially the ones where you are not able to control what is thrown at you – the ones where you feel incapable of determining the future, be reminded to use the make-up kit to enhance the circumstance. Live in the moment and don't dread the outcome because you will be around people who want your success, those that won't judge you and will only offer support. You will have established goals in your life and have something wonderful to look forward to as a new day dawns. You will wake each new day with an affirmation to get the day started. It may be "I am loved" or "No weapon formed against me will prosper." You will be happy for the success of others, and experience their gladness as if it were your own. You will have faith that each and every moment will become better. You will look into your heart and forgive those who have caused harm. You will give of yourself and your time. You will learn to control your negative emotions through your motivation and recognition of your beliefs. You will live a thankful life, a life where opportunities for pleasure will be created every morning.

Have you ever asked yourself, "What do I have to be grateful for?" There is an old Chinese proverb I want you to inscribe on the outside of your "make-up bag". I took the liberty of paraphrasing it. *"A young woman was sad that she didn't have a pair of Manolo Blahnik shoes, and then she became thankful she had on shoes when she saw a woman with no feet."*

I would like you to create a symbolic *Live a Thankful Life Make-Up Bag*. When you see the "make-up product", remember the skill, and practice them. Place in the bag, Love yourself, Positive Thoughts, Goals, Positive People, Affirmations, Appreciation for the Success of Others, Faith, Forgiveness, Giving and Emotion Control.

To be thankful, you must find the delight of being. The tools above help you to center yourself into a way of life that offers peace without the commotion of doubt. When you live with the assurance that all is well, it is and you can see the things in life in which you are thankful. I am thankful that my daughter is not only my child, but also my counselor and friend. I am thankful that I learned patience from my husband and self-empowerment from my mother. Life is good and God is great all the time. Thank you for allowing me the opportunity to share my thoughts and advice. May God bless you and keep you close to His heart. "I am thankful." That is your new mantra.

ABOUT THE AUTHOR

BOBBIE CRUDUP QUALLS

Bobbie Crudup Qualls is an Educator with thirty plus years of experience in leadership. She received her Rank 1 certification in Administration Leadership and Masters of Education Degree in Guidance and Counseling from University of Louisville.

She served as a Distinguished Educator from Department of Education (1998-2000) and retired as a Distinguished Leader (Consultant) from Jefferson County Public School. She holds a certification in Organizational Leadership (ZOL) from Zeta Phi Beta Sorority. Because of her educational leadership and services in the school system and community, Ms. Qualls has been awarded numerous recognitions and honors: NAACP High School Teacher of the Year, Great Lakes Region: State Director of the Year (Zeta Phi Beta Sorority), Woman of the Year (Zeta Phi Beta Sorority), Finer Womanhood Award (Zeta Phi Beta Sorority), March of Dimes Service Award, Distinguished Educator Cadre Award, and Outstanding Woman of America Award.

Her goal for over twenty five years has been to become an Educational and Leadership Consultant. She hopes to start an organization and coach / empower young ladies to develop themselves into exemplary leaders who serve humanity

Ms. Qualls is a member of Community Missionary Baptist Church, Educational Advisor of Newburg Youth Council (NYC), an exuberant member of the Professional Woman Network (PWN), member of Women in School Administration (WSA), and a Life Member of Zeta Phi Beta Sorority, where she served as Kentucky State Director 2002-2008. She is a humble Partner of Crudup -Ward Day Care and Activity Center, founded by his sister, Annie Crudup-Ward Lowery.

Contact:
Bobbie Qualls
8212 Thornwood Road
Louisville, KY
quallsbf@aol.com

TWO

TEN WAYS TO LOVE YOURSELF

By Bobbie Crudup Qualls

Love is the universal language and people all over the world want to love and (to) be loved. Even an infant learns very early expressions of love: a smile, a nod, a gentle touch, a warm bath, and moments of bonding with parents... Unfortunately, too many times, as we grow older, society and the media send messages that show us through life changing situations that we are not smart enough, or petite enough, or good enough or loved enough. As we dwell on our imperfections, we begin to believe what is told directly as well as indirectly to us. Well, before we sink into "self pities remember, God didn't create junk...

As this chapter progresses, I hope you reflect deeply on loving yourself spiritually, mentally and physically. **Stay with me while I share with you Ten Ways to Love Yourself.**

Embrace Biblical Love.

God is Love! God loves you! *"God so loved the world that He gave His Only begotten Son, that whoever believes in Him should not perish but have everlasting life."* (John 3:16 NKJV) What a powerful truth that sustains you to love YOURSELF!

Many of you readers were reared within a family that embraced religion. Your devotion to God took on weekly (or more frequent) trips to church—reading scripture, singing Gospels, praying and meditating, and AMEN! AMEN! AMENing the preacher's sermons. You received a foundation to know God and to obey God's commands. You learned about the greatest commandment (Matthew 22:36-38 NKJV). And as you embraced biblical love, you understood that the Ten Commandments reflect Jesus' three great commands. You were taught principles of right versus wrong, truth versus lies, and a knowledge of our Supreme Being called God. Embrace and pursue this selfless and unconditional biblical love and you will strive to see yourself as God sees you: **loved.**

Now it's **your** turn: Read 1 Corinthians 13, "The Love Chapter." State or describe 3-5 characteristics of what love IS/or what love is NOT.

1. Love is/is not _____

2. Love is/is not _____

3. Love is/is not _____

4. Love is/is not _____

5. Love is/is not _____

Can you see how you can love yourself by incorporating these characteristics in your own life toward yourself? Now you're beginning to see how you can start loving yourself biblically!

Empower Self to Accept Self.

How do you view yourself? What do you really see and hear when you look in the full-length mirror? Do you see yourself loving who you see? As you focus on your outer appearance, pause and pierce deeply into your inner most being. Encourage yourself as you analyze your self-evaluation and discard the self-criticism 'record'. Check out your strengths, and search for those unique character traits and talents. Inhale deeply and exhale slowly as you accept and love this beautiful person created by God.

Serve Humanity.

Dr. Martin Luther King, Jr. said "…anybody can serve. You don't have to have a college degree to serve; you only need a heart full of grace, a soul generated by love." Each of you has that soul generated by love; you have a heart full of compassion, and as you serve others, your heart overflows with joy. This joyous heart loves and respects you and expresses its love by serving humanity.

Observe these 'Taking Action Loving and Serving' suggestions:

- Donate blood. Someone is always injured or sick and in need of blood.

- Serve as a role model. Teach our youth or be an advisor for a youth organization group.

- Provide time, resources, and services to disabled individuals, veterans.

- Visit the shut-ins, hospital patients, nursing homes (share your time, service, etc.).

- Be a support system for military families, children of prisoners, disaster victims.

- Support children ministry with time, resources, services.

- Be a beacon of hope, a shining light for others.

- Donate and volunteer to charity: Salvation Army, Disabled Veterans, Cedar Lake, American Council for Blind, Wayside Mission, etc.

- Join a group (organization) and serve or help an organization implement its mission.

    As you love and serve in truth and action, you will see compassion and joy multiply in your life. When you embrace those in need, you will also be embracing who YOU are!

Lavish Your Body.

    Whether I am at the Paradise Island of Kauai, Hawaii, the white sand beaches in Montego Bay, Jamaica, or at the Z-SPA in Louisville, Kentucky, I reserve a day to LAVISH my body by heading to a spa…a serene sanctuary where healing hands soothe my body, mind, and spirit. I embrace myself, realizing that these trips enhance my well-being.

    Let's take a peek into a 'vacation spa journey.' GO AHEAD! YOU DESERVE IT!

- Relaxation exercises/quick shower: Oh, my! It soothes, relaxes, and cleanses.

- Body masks: Use body masks made of almond oil or rose essential oil.

- Caribbean full body massage: This conditions skin and moisturizes with lush Caribbean botanical oils.

- Serenity bath: Yes, like that Epsom salt, Bath & Body Works, candles, and music.

- Romantic sunset sailing dinner: Dine and dance—Wow! Love is in the air!

Echo Affirmations Daily.

Affirmation, to me, is a straight-forward, specific, positive statement which, when constantly echoed, will change and reinforce thinking patterns on a subconscious level. That's Right! I want you to start affirming yourself and echoing who you are right now! S2 P4 ... straight forward, specific, positive, personal, powerful statements representing you and written in the present tense.

Reflect on the following chart. These affirmations represent a positive self-reflection. Check the columns that identify how you best view yourself. (You're right! The amount of checks you have in the last two columns indicate how positively you see yourself.)

Affirmation: Rate yourself as accurately as possible.	Never	Sometimes	Always
I am loved by God.			
Intelligent, enthusiastic, unique . . . that's me!			
My heavenly Father guides me and teaches me daily.			

My body is my partner . . I love it and take care of it.			
I forgive and let go!			
I respect myself and accept myself wholeheartedly.			
My smile is contagious; I'm passinzg it on!			
I'm embracing the inner child in me.			
Serving humanity is a joy . . . that's me!			
I love God, humanity, myself.			
I am a generous giver! Freely, I give.			
I am high on life . . . not drugs, not alcohol, not tobacco.			
I passionately communicate my needs and my desires to others.			
My positive attitude brings confidence and significance.			

Now it's YOUR turn! Get emotionally charged up! Write five affirmations using positive, powerful, personal statements about you. Use the present tense.

1. _____

2. _____

3. _____

4. _____

5. _____

Now VISUALIZE them! BELIEVE them! Echo them! LOVE YOURSELF!

Dump the Negativity.

Do you view the glass as half full or half empty? Are you empowering others to drain you of your energies, time, future, or life? Are you embracing a negative thinking pattern? Sometimes we are the worst critics we have! Our self-doubts are so prevalent that we really don't need others to bring us down emotionally; we do that very well to ourselves! My friend Jennifer used to call herself "duh-me" for her mistakes in what she thought was a cover-up or a putdown. She is in no way stupid, but her self-labeling was eroding her own self-image! After she took a Bible study called *"Me, Myself, and Lies"* developed by Jennifer Rothschild, she learned that condemnation brings destruction; she realized she was actually destroying her self-image! She later acclaimed, "If we love ourselves, we will not believe lies that are destructive to our natural selves."

Well, do you hang around with people who are constantly complaining about their lives, their jobs, their families, and their health? The ironic thing about negativity is that it SPREADS like wildfire. We seem to commiserate with those who seemingly have it "bad." What, conversely, happens to you when you share time with friends who laugh and share joyful thoughts about their lives? Can you remember a time when you laughed so hard that you cried? How were your spirits then? How did you feel about life/yourself? Luke 6:45 tells us, *"For out of the overflow of his heart his mouth speaks."* Which group of your friends/associates has the joy in their hearts? How joyful and content is YOUR heart? Embrace the joy of life…that is part of showing your love for yourself!

Point to ponder: We must learn how to respond to negativity and how to change negative thinking patterns. Explain the phrase, Love yourself by changing the Negative Thinking Pattern.

Share a Smile / Share a 'Belly' Laugh

"Hi, Lady with the beautiful smile." I'd heard this phrase many times, but didn't pay much attention to it until I started observing the smiles, frowns, the scowls, the grimaces on other people's faces. So loosen up those facial muscles and smile as you love yourself.

Speaking of laughter, how much do you laugh? Or even smile? People smile only 35% as much as they think they do (Robin Thompson, **Know** Stress to No Stress)

- Smiling costs us nothing; it brings joy to others; it is contagious: Pass it on!

- Smiling and laughter are part of our basic makeup. The average preschooler laughs 400 times a day. That number drops to only 15 times a day by the time people reach age 35!

- Laughter is actually good for us and it requires no prescription co-pay! It releases endorphins, a chemical ten times more powerful than the pain-relieving drug morphine.

We were CREATED to smile / laugh. Exchange a smile and a gesture of love is expressed.

Take Care of Your Health.

"Beloved, I pray that in all respects you may prosper and be in good health, just as your soul prospers." –(3 John 1:2)

As women, we sometimes forget how important good health and nutrition are until health begins to fail us. We realize that sick people must be treated and we must manage chronic conditions. Nonetheless, it is crucial that we be informed when it comes to preventive health. Be informed about the following actions, which can promote good health:

1. **Annual Physician Visits (which include screening tests and immunizations):** When you go to your primary care physician, take your screening chart with you (website: www.womenshealth.gov, click on Publications: Screening Tests and Immunizations guidelines for women). Make a list, ask your questions and discuss those issues. Be sure to mention changes that you do not understand. Remember, you are paying for direct, personal, medical answers to your questions. It is also crucial that you visit other medical specialists (i.e. dentist, ophthalmologist, gynecologist, etc.)

2. **Good Nutrition/Vitamins:** Women want to maintain a healthy weight, a good night's sleep, a properly functioning body, a high energy level, a healthy heart, and strong bones. It all starts with a healthy diet. Place a copy of A Daily Food Pyramid (www.

mypyramid.gov) on your refrigerator and use it DAILY. Find out what is recommended each day, and remember that a balanced diet incorporates all the food groups.

Don't forget your vitamins; however, be careful when taking herbal supplements. Talk with doctor about which vitamins and/or herbal supplements may benefit you.

3. **Consistent Regular Physical Activity:** Move that bod'! 30 minutes of strenuous activities 3 – 5 days weekly will show both your body and your cardiovascular system that you love them!

4. **Explore the "Search Your Heart Program."** Research and utilize this community based educational program, which is divided into three areas: Heart Disease and Stroke, Nutrition, and Physical Activity. **Visit webMD.com for information and slideshows on all types of medical issues.**

Remember: You think of your heart when it comes to relationships. Let's not forget "about a broken heart" when it comes to your health. Love your heart as you love yourself!

NOW IT'S YOUR TURN: Identify three ways you are going to love yourself by promoting good health.

1. _____

2. _____

3. _____

Grab That Stress and Manage It.

Wow! You're facing a pressure-filled week. Perhaps a conflict is brewing with colleagues; a major project is due; a relationship is crumbling; a loved one is experiencing an unexpected illness. Life may have tossed you a lemon this week, but DON'T PANIC! Love yourself as you drink your lemonade and de-stress.

1. **Relax:** Positive affirmations will relax your body and mind.

2. **Moment of Peace:** Pray, mediate or read scripture. Allow God to fight your battle.

3. **Practice Music Therapy:** Provides a positive state of mind (relaxes and calms you).

4. **Dance:** Move to the beat of a favorite song (i.e. "The Twist" by Chubby Checker)

5. **Smell:** Tuck 100% essential oils into your desk drawer: savor the sweet fragrances.

6. **Dial Up:** Call a supportive friend and connect with positive conversation.

7. **Ballgame Time:** Hit the gymnasium and Scream! Scream! Scream!

8. **Cultivate:** Plants flowers or trees. Tension melts away as you dig into the earth.

Soak Up Nature.

Have you heard the terms *green exercise, green prescriptions,* or even *ecotherapy?* Doctors are finding many health benefits from nature, including reductions in stress, depression and aggression, both in children and adults. Both *green exercise and ecotherapy* refer to the benefits of soaking up nature as part of a loving, healthy lifestyle. *Green prescriptions* refers to doctors giving "prescriptions" to their patients to spend time outside, in nature. What an ideal way to love yourself in the company of God's creation!

Living on 44 acres of land in the country during my childhood, I took nature walks every day with my sisters and brother. I loved being surrounded by nature as I worked and played in the sun during the day and stared at the moon and stars at night. I relish returning home today to visit family and soak up an abundance of God's created nature.

So, indulge yourself. Improve your health and boost your spirit as you walk along the countryside. Smell the beautiful wildflowers (cardinal flowers, goldenrod, pine lily and hibiscus), taste the delicious plums, peaches, grapes, and pears as you stop at the spring for a cup of God's provided nature water. Enjoy the fresh air as you watch the colorful butterflies fluttering in the beautiful flower garden. Listen to the sounds of frogs and crickets. Notice the deer leap across the yard and observe the hummingbirds, purple martins and blue birds feed their young. Leap into the pond for a quick swim (or catch some fish in the lake). Stop by and chat with a neighbors as they work in their garden. You dare not leave the country without receiving 'loads' of veggies, nuts and fruits. Love yourself as you bask in nature's surroundings. Enjoy!

Note: Echo through affirmations and implement these ten ways to love yourself spiritually, mentally, and physically. As you travel on this journey called Life, **you may become bruised. However you will also discover that with God's grace and mercy, you will not be broken. Rejoice!** You got it! You are loved!

Recommended Books / Websites

The Charles F. Stanley Life Principles Bible by Charles F. Stanley

Know Stress to No Stress by Robin Thompson

Me, Myself and Lies by Priscilla Rothschild

www.vitalaffirmations.com (Positive Thinking to Manifest Change)

www.webMD.slideshows (Medical Slideshows subjects A-Z)

Dedication to Mom (Catherine Moore Lovelady Crudup October 21, 1931-July 21, 2008)

Thanks for your legacy of love...

ABOUT THE AUTHOR

MAVIS PEMBERTON

Mavis Pemberton is the Founder and CEO of Victorious Consulting, Inc. She is passionate about helping others *Reach Up* to achieve their full potential in business, ministry and their pursuit of a healthy lifestyle. *We Reach Out* to serve you.

She has over 25 years experience in Human Resources, and has managed several functions in Fortune 500 companies. She provides an integrated mix of customizable services in the areas of human resources, wellness solutions; grant writing assistance targeted to start-ups, small to midsize companies, non-profit and faith-based organizations.

Her responsibility for benefits administration fanned her passion for health and wellness, a critical tool to reduce healthcare costs, and to create a culture of proactive, preventative care in all organizations. This has led to her pursuit of additional training and certifications to make a difference in the lives of others. She is a graduate of Sacred Heart University with Bachelors, and an MBA in business administration. She is a member of the Professional Woman Network (PWN) and a certified trainer. She has acquired various certifications through such organizations as the American Management Association and the Society for Human Resources Management.

As a Nutraceutical Consultant and Transition Lifestyle Coach she has the ability and knowledge to blend these services holistically to deliver comprehensive wellness solutions. These solutions impact all aspects of small to medium sized businesses in the areas of healthcare, employee productivity and morale. She is currently working with churches within the state of Connecticut to establish wellness ministries within their organizations. Her focus has been to speak at women's events, and share the good news about their empowerment to take charge of their health.

She is available for speaking engagements at Women's celebrations and Youth events.

Contact:
Mavis Pemberton
Victorious Consulting, Inc.
Milford, CT 06460
(800) 910-1893
mavis@victoriousconsulting.org
www.victoriousconsulting.org

THREE

VICTIM TO VICTORY

By Mavis Pemberton

"The capacity for hope is the most significant fact of life. It provides human beings with a sense of destination and the energy to get started."
—Norman Cousins

This is an intense subject, but it becomes the microscope that we each must use to examine our mindset and willingness to transform our lives from victim to victory. Webster's dictionary defines a victim as "one who is harmed by or made to suffer from an act, circumstance, agency or condition." We are a society proliferated by victims. We are victims of our culture which is responsible for our mindset. It has become our brand of identity, and I would dare say, some of us even wear it as a badge of honor. We have become victims to ourselves because our thoughts and words do not line up, and our lives reflect the disconnection. We are victims of divorce, financial ruin, layoffs, false accusations, poverty, racism, loss of loved ones, and the list goes on and on.

There is, however, no greater victim than that of a child who is molested and sexually abused by a predator disguised as an uncle or relative. This unspeakable crime and evil begins the process of self-destruction, low self-esteem and self-worth for most young girls and boys, unless there is an early intervention. As I expound on this subject, you can examine your own life and make some critical decisions.

Questions for Reflection:

Where do you see yourself?

_____

_____

_____

Are you truly a victim?

_____

_____

_____

Are you playing the "blame game" because you refuse to take responsibility for your own actions?

_____

_____

_____

Do you believe that life owes you something because of where you were born, the color of your skin, your family status or lack thereof?

_____

_____

_____

If you answered yes to any of those questions, what can you do differently to begin the healing process, and to create a new vision for yourself?

_____

_____

_____

Let me provide some insights by sharing a few anecdotes about the lives of three women I interviewed, and a few practical steps to guide you through this most difficult period. There is hope, and therefore, there is victory.

Patty was seven years old when the molestation began by an uncle who was trusted, and unsupervised when he visited the home. This led to her sexual exploits with boys, and later at the age of thirteen to prostitution. Patty had discovered the power of using her body to get money and whatever she wanted. She had made a conscious decision to travel on this path, and did not want a detour. Patty was raised in a good home with a hard-working mother and other siblings. She was rebellious and wanted to experience life on her terms. Patty's story is one that is intense, filled with danger and disbelief as she journeyed deeper into a life filled with self-destruction, cocaine, heroin and alcohol. She was often physically abused by men, threatened with bodily harm, thrown out of moving vehicles, shot at, imprisoned several times for larceny and written off as lost. She was fearless and faced death on many occasions, but she was determined to live life on the street, even when she was homeless and slept in the Salvation Army bins in the winter months. Deep in her core, she knew right from wrong and would refuse to use drugs in front of children. She herself was a mother at fifteen, but had given up her daughter to be raised by an aunt.

What was the turning point in her life? What are the nuggets you can glean from this story that will change how you see yourself and bring hope into your life?

Deep in her heart, Patty believed that there was and is a God who loved her. She believed that she would get out of this life of drugs and prostitution. She constantly was told that she would amount to nothing by her pimps, boyfriends and others in her life. Her cocaine and heroin habit kept her constantly high, and she did any and everything to support the habit. She recalled the moment when she spoke the words declaring that she would get out, and be happily married with two kids. Patty recalled the summer night when she heard a voice calling her name and knew it was the voice of God. When she answered, she made the decision to change her life, but the road to victory was not an easy one. She had spoken the words into the atmosphere, and declared that she would be victorious one day.

There were many twists and turns that occurred in her life. She recalled living in a drug infested motel, and hearing a knock at the door on a Sunday morning. It was some people from a nearby church inviting her to church. They brought clothes to her and helped her get ready. She went to church still high on the drugs, but sat in the last row. Patty's deliverance and path to healing began when she made the decision to surrender to the Lord. Her healing has been a journey that took her in and out of prison, but away from the drugs, alcohol and prostitution. She wanted to be in prison. It was in prison that she obtained her GED, and certificates in other subject areas. God's grace met her there, and through prison she found her way back to Him.

Today, Patty is a strong, anointed woman of God, happily married with two kids. She was also reunited with her daughter with whom she has a very close relationship. Her ministry and passion is to serve God with diligence, unwavering commitment, and to rescue other women from the streets. She restores them to wholeness, teaches them self-love and the love of God.

Let's meet Annie, a very attractive, cultured, and mature woman who was always adored and loved by her parents. She was the first child to be born after four miscarriages, and was therefore protected and cherished. As an only girl, and the oldest of three brothers, she had a very close relationship with her mother. As she grew older, boys were very attracted to her and vice versa. She later had two kids out of wedlock, but received assistance from her mom. She went through a rough phase as she migrated to Connecticut to live while her kids were in South Carolina. Later, she was able to bring her kids to Connecticut.

Life changed for Annie when she met the man of her dreams. Jimmy was the love of her life and they had twenty wonderful years together. During this time, Annie began to care for her mom who was a diabetic. She was a woman of faith and believed that her mom's leg would not be amputated, and witnessed the healing. When she returned to Connecticut, there were periods of challenges with her mom's health, but she continued to live for another two years after this healing. Her mom later experienced a heart attack and died. She wanted to move on, and died before Annie and her husband could get there. This loss was the beginning of a process which led to depression and thoughts of suicide. Within nine months of losing her mother, Annie needed to have a complete hysterectomy. She was still grieving the loss of her mother and questioned why God would allow her to be healed only to take her away. The next year, Jimmy would suffer a massive heart attack and die. To compound all of this, Annie began to lose the pigmentation in her hands, face and neck. This was all extremely trying as she cried every day and went into an even deeper depression.

Her battle was directly with God as she questioned His very existence, and the substance of her beliefs. Through it all, she still reached out to God as friends led her to a non-denominational church with unusual rituals that she had never experienced. Today, through many personal encounters with our Lord, Annie's faith is stronger than ever as she surrendered her life completely to Him. She said that she sold out to Him. As long as she went to church, she stopped crying. Over time, He removed the pain of her physical and personal losses. Her story is one of restoration and discovery as she truly learned who Jehovah was and is. She is a powerful woman of God, and a strong intercessor who truly loves the Lord and is not ashamed to share her testimony of healing and deliverance from depression and suicidal tendencies. Her testimony has been shared with hundreds of people over the years and she is respected for her walk with God and the anointing upon her life.

Not everyone has transcended the victim to victory mentality. Amy, a woman who has only begun the journey, still has a long way to go. She is a victim of domestic violence, rape and imprisonment in a foreign country. Her arrival back in the USA is truly a miracle of God. Her belief sustained her as she believed that she would return to the USA and to the arms of her family. Unfortunately, the family is not fully embracing her arrival. The challenge here is the expectation she has that they should take care of her and her four children. Yes, she was a victim, but has not been set free of the victim mindset.

When you choose to depend on others and to wear the badge of a victim, you attract the most unscrupulous characters like a magnet because of the type of energy you exude. She has questioned why the wrong people are constantly seeking her out. This is all part of the journey, but we encourage you to be introspective and look at your own mindset. There must be recognition and acknowledgement of the changes needed as healing begins in the heart. You have to know you need deliverance of your past so you can change your present and embrace your future. When Amy is ready to let go of her anger, bitterness, resentment and to forgive her husband and her family, we will see a change in her and her life. There are key elements to be learned, even from her story. She has arrived at one point, but now needs to begin to travel on a path of faith and total surrender. Fear keeps her looking back, but I believe she will focus on moving forward when the fire gets hot enough.

My story is one of joy in the early years of my childhood in Trinidad, but that soon changed when my father left home. That change at the age of eleven meant the beginning of a very tortured existence for me as my childhood became one of physical abuse. I am the oldest of three and the only girl. As the first born, I was responsible for the state of my mother's life, at least those were the statements made during my physical beatings. My inner strength came from experiences with the Lord at the age of ten when I gave my life to Him at a Billy Graham crusade. I knew the Lord and knew I could call on Him.

I was driven to achieve excellence in everything I did in school and sports, but nothing pleased her. There came a point when she no longer mattered to me, but I was driven by something on the inside. I know now that He is my helper, but back then, I only knew that when I spoke to my heavenly father, my prayers were answered. When I was offered the opportunity to immigrate to the United States, I immediately said yes. This opened the door to freedom, but also created other challenges

I had to face as a teenager with strangers as relatives in Brooklyn. I never considered myself a victim, but dreamed of my life and how I wanted it to be.

Of course, there are always patterns that we unconsciously are drawn to and I unfortunately experienced the psychological abuse that surfaced later in my marriage. Internal strength and determination provided the elements of the vision for my future. I survived through a difficult divorce, financial ruin, the loss of my home, and being a single mother of two. I had the support and prayers of my closest friends who are my sisters. Prayers and my faith kept me focused on a different outcome for my life. It is never easy because you have to just go through the fire and the storm. Sometimes I have cried out, Lord, this is not just any storm, but this is a tsunami. How do you survive major losses in your life, betrayal, and still avoid becoming or thinking of yourself as a victim? From a world view, I was a victim, but from God's view, I was an overcomer. Victory is always a process and a journey. We sometimes take detours because we want to fix it, but then you have to go back to the crossroads and do it all over again, choosing a path until you get it right.

"Wait on the Lord: be of good courage, and He shall strengthen your heart: wait, I say on the Lord."—Psalms 27:14 (NIV)

We will explore some of the practical recommendations that can be applied to your life. You can walk out of every situation when you are ready. We have the power of life and death. Our choice of life is always the unknown, but this is where we must trust in Him. Death and darkness are always your present situation, and what you are most comfortable with. You don't need to be around people describing your situation and reliving every bleak, dark moment. You need a prescription for your future. Victory, according to Webster, is "any successful struggle against an opponent or obstacle."

For each heading, identify your thoughts, and where you are according to the description outlined in the following statements. You should experience the following to successfully transform your life.

1. **Change Your Mindset:** *"And be not conformed to this world: but be ye transformed by the renewing of your mind, that ye may prove what is that good, and acceptable, and perfect will of God."*—Romans 12: 2 (KJV)

When your mind has been renewed, you can then accept who you are in Christ and the love He has for you. You must take control of your mind. Guard your mind by focusing on reading His Word, daily prayer and alone time with Him.

_____

_____

_____

_____

_____

_____

2. **Forgiveness:** You must first forgive others who have wronged you, but most importantly, you must forgive yourself. When you forgive, you are choosing to love and release all the bitterness. You must forget about the past. Paul said, *"...forgetting those things which are behind...."* He is talking about a constant, deliberate discarding

of all your past thoughts and defeats. *"I press toward the mark....."*
—Philippians 3: 13 - 14 (KJV)

Recognize there are no breakthroughs without the battles you have been through.

Who do you need to forgive? Can you prepare a list that you can pray about and ask God to release you from these soul ties that bind you to this person or persons.

_____

_____

_____

_____

_____

_____

3. **Faith/Belief:** A belief in the one supreme God, Jehovah, is essential to your healing. Without Him, you cannot get out of the darkness into His light. You are blinded by the depth of your past. Believe that there is greatness within you.

_____

_____

_____

_____

_____

_____

4. **Surrender:** This is not always easy, as you have been in control or controlled by others. Surrendering to God is essential so that He can begin the healing process and cover you with His blood.

How do you surrender, stop trying to be superwoman and do it all yourself? Just let Him be God. Learn to trust Him for everything. He is your Father; just take the time to know Him.

_____

_____

_____

_____

_____

_____

5. **Pray Daily:** *"Jesus rose early to pray. "*—Mark 1:35. Prayer keeps you connected and is your lifeline. You can follow the light. Jesus says, *"He is the light of the world and that you shall not walk in darkness, but have the light of life."*—John 8:12

_____

_____

_____

_____

_____

_____

6. **Create a Vision:** What do you want the rest of your life to be? Speak the words over your life. You are responsible for creating your new future. All the prayers will not help you unless you speak it and believe it. Focus on the areas of spiritual, physical, emotional, and financial health, as well as relationships. Be specific.

"Write the vision and make it plain…"—Habakkuk 2:2 (NIV)

_____

_____

_____

_____

_____

_____

It is important to wake up with the intention to have and live a victorious life. You can be whatever God wants you to be. You can have all that He wants you to have. Don't become submerged in the aspects of our culture that will stifle your creativity and your freedom. Remember, *"Beloved, I wish above all things that you may prosper and be in health, even as your soul prospers."*—3 John 2 (NIV)

Renegotiate those relationships, and evaluate who enters into your inner circle. Can they support your walk from victim to victory? If not, walk away from them. Or are they trying to keep you tied to your past situations, emotions and mindset? Continue to acknowledge responsibility for your life and take back your personal power by force.

Dedication: *Thank you Prophetess for sharing and letting God use you mightily. And to my big sister for being there for me through many storms, and to my new sister who has just begun this walk. There is much more to tell, but those testimonies are yours to write.*

Recommended Reading
The Holy Bible

Commanding Your Morning by Dr. Cindy Trimm

Battlefield of the Mind by Joyce Meyers

Notes:

ABOUT THE AUTHOR

Ms. Charlene Sills

Charlene Sills CEO of Alpha 2 Omega International Institute. LLC. She conducts seminars on Teen Self Image, Beginners Etiquette for Teens and The Motivated Young. She also holds full coaching seminars and empowerment classes on The Authentic Woman, Avoiding Toxic Relationships, First Impressions, The Superwoman Syndrome, Customer Service and The Professional Woman. Ms. Sills is certified by the Professional Woman's Network as a Professional Coach and Seminar Consultant.

Charlene's vast experience in business includes over 17 years as a manager in a fortune 500 company as well as a philanthropist and entrepreneur. As CEO of Alpha 2 Omega International Institute she offers her services to holds seminars and wellness classes to churches, businesses and youth organizations looking to educate, motivate and enhance its core structure. Ms. Sills is an accomplished author, Member of Toastmasters and holds a B. A. in Business Management from Strayer University. Charlene has mentored young women, motivated young men and celebrated diversity among employees of all ages in Corporate America.

Books:
- Co-Author - Bruised But Not Broken (PWN 2010)
- Co-Author - Raising Healthy Children in an Unhealthy World (PWN 2010)
- Co-Author - The Teen Handbook For Self Confidence (PWN 2010)

Certified as a consultant by PWN-Holds seminars in the following areas:
- Women's issues
- First Impressions
- The Superwoman Syndrome
- Teen Empowerment
- Teen Etiquette
- Improving Customer Service
- Diversity
- Assertive - vs - Aggressive

Professional Affiliations:
Consortium of Information and Telecommunication Executives.
Cambridge Who's Who.

Contact:
P.O. Box 210
Lumberton NJ, 08048
(609) 781-2433
Alpha2OmegaIntl@aol.com

FOUR

THE IMPORTANCE OF SISTERHOOD

By Charlene Sills

If you walk into any Hallmark© store, you will see that Sisterhood is a celebration for women who are in your life on purpose. Whatever your higher power may be, you have been magnetically drawn to specific people during the course of your life for one reason or another. Forming and maintaining a good network of sisters is as easy as ABC. You can take your existing network of familiar associates and see where they fall into the grand scheme of potential sisterhood members. For the next few pages, I am going to go through my sisterhood network and give you some pointers that will help you form bonds that will last and thrive over time. Now, I am not going to tell you I have a sister for every letter of the alphabet. What would be the point? The initials stated represent the first letter of their names. What I will do is help you find your own alphabet of sisters among the friends you already have. The success of a tight knit Sisterhood is more than just what

YOU get out of it. It is equally important to know what you have to continually *PUT INTO* it.

 My two 'A' girls are not a big part of my life now, but they are an important part of my growth and life development. Both of them are younger than I and are experiencing events that I have already lived through. (Try staying connected to a few people who you no longer see on a daily/weekly basis.) Reach out to them periodically and see how they are doing and what has been going on in their lives. You should try to keep younger sisters in your hood to keep you from getting ahead of yourself. Forgetting them may mean forgetting events in your past that have helped shape the foundation of your adulthood. Don't forget where you came from. Your experiences can be life lessons for the generations behind you.

Your younger friends are _____ ,_____ and similar to the path you walked before, they are _____.

 My 'B' is my Queen. She is the woman who gave me life, **My Mommy;** she continues to give me inspiration. She has said that only God can show her how to love others and I am blessed in abundance to have had a guide like her show me right from wrong at an early age. She taught me respect for myself and others, love of simple things, and a yearning to see what else can be done with life. She is the first person to show me the importance of sisterhoods by surrounding herself with strong women to whom she entrusted her most important jewel (me). I quickly learned how to define the relationships my mother had with other women. Follow along and see if this brings back memories. "This is Mrs. Smith. This is Ms. Jones. This is Mama Green. This is Sarah Jenkins." With just a simple introduction, you have just been taught the respect level you better have for all of your mother's sisterhood members. Hidden in that was the knowledge of who has already been given authority to whip your behind if she saw you doing something you were not supposed to be doing (Mama Green). With life's twist and turns, you may not have your mother around in your life, but there should be an older adult woman whose strength you draw from and who reminds you that life is different now because of the foundation she taught you when you were younger.

Your Queen is _____ and God gave you to her for a reason. REMEMBER IT!

 My 'D' friend is a fellow entrepreneur and co-worker. We have worked for a Fortune 500 corporation for many years but have only worked together for the last nine. We have survived expansions and decreases and support each other almost daily to ease the uncertainties. I aspire to be a sincere source of knowledge, encouragement, motivation and assistance as she takes steps to solidify her place among successful business women in today's society. I have to stay personally educated on various small business-related topics and periodically ask her, "Did you know……?" Now if you don't have a 'D' friend that you can encourage to start her own business, check your mental rolodex and see if there may be a 'D' friend that falls into the "*I would love to work along side her doing (whatever)*" category.

Your entrepreneur friend is _____
_____ and she has started a _____.
If not, how about "if I could, I would love to go into business with her
doing _____."

My three 'K' girls are as different from me as night from day, yet as similar to me as grains of rice. Two of them are married, hard working women with high levels of education and diverse professional backgrounds. One has grown children (like me) and we were there when the other 'K' began her introduction into motherhood. My two 'Ks' and I get together at least twice every year. Everything "girlie girl" is done during these visits and I get great satisfaction in reminding myself that I am 100% woman. Our itinerary includes massages, facials, shopping, shows, dancing, workouts and above all else, fine dining and endless laughs and conversation. Our diverse occupations provide a variety of topics to indulge in. You would be surprised that despite our differences, it is our similarities that bind us into the strongly bonded sisterhood that we cherish.

Your travel sisters are _____ and
_____. I encourage you to promise yourself
to make a point to meet with them regularly and enjoy an outing once
every _____ so that you can let our hair down or take it
off completely.

My other 'K' sister girl is a world apart from the other 'K' girls. Again, she is very intelligent and outspoken, but this 'K' sister is a REAL SISTA. She is a DIVA FASHIONISTA. My 'K' girl keeps me on top of all the entertainment news, the latest fashion trends, and all the celebrity gossip. This 'K' girl (as with all of my sisters network) would be comfortable in any social situation. Diva 'K' attends shows, movies, parties and conferences with me. Within minutes she can spot a fashion do versus a fashion don't. She has shown me the meaning of retail therapy and that the height of your heels depends on who you are trying to get back at or piss off, not how short you are. (Spoken like the true 5 feet tall women that we are!)

Your Diva sister is _____
_____ and she has the inside scoop on _____
_____ that keeps you in the know.

I have three sisters that are my daughters and genuine gifts from God. I would have accomplished nothing and would have gotten nowhere without them. Expounding individually, 'T' (the oldest) has taken my outspoken characteristic and magnified it by 1000. She wants to believe she is an outcast in society, but has come to the realization that she fits perfectly into the fabric of our lives. 'J' is the middle child and has mirrored my ability to face situations head on and take full ownership of the outcome. She can tell you no and have you waiting on a reason that is not forthcoming. "No" doesn't always have to come with an explanation, but don't cross her because it may come with some expletives. 'W' is the baby and she has taken all the love showered on her by the rest of us and reflected it back at us in a way to make us see each other in a higher standard of life and acceptance.

Collectively, they are my reasons to smile every single day. I shed a tear just thinking about the love these three jewels have given me. No topic is taboo with them. I raised them to respectfully challenge my ways and they have shown me that love starts at home. I thank God that He has allowed me enough time on this earth to see them become adult women. His guidance through me has made them my Best Female Friends.

Your BFF (list your daughters)

_____

_____

_____

 My 'M' is my rock. She is my grounded, married, level headed sister girl who's council I seek feverishly when I need to focus. She pushes me, encourages me, motivates me, and on several occasions knows how to reel me in when I spin away from my core center. My 'M' never lets me be satisfied with skating by. She is the first to kick me in my butt when I want to sit back and let life happen around me. 'M' will ask me what is going in my life and why I have not thought up a new venture. I am less afraid to fail because 'M' has taught me to press on. To her, everything is possible if you truly want it and never pass up the opportunity to do better and elevate your status above where you currently are. In listening to her conversation with others, I have found that this is an unselfish trait that is deep within her. Several people seek her council and she will quickly say, "You should try that." Although we are different in many ways, intellectually she is my mirror. I do my reality check through her eyes.

Your motivational friend is _____ and in her you see your _____ .

Let me digress from my alphabet for just a second to share this bit of information. An important lesson I learned while taking a good look at my sisterhood was how to meet your sister girl friends on *THEIR* level. You should and will have sisters in your hood who are more affluent than you, more educated than you, more spiritual than you and more social than you. You have to not only allow them their differences, but you can draw strength from their differences in your own life. Some will be food and entertainment buddies where others just need a listening ear to talk things out. Some will help you bless your home and mourn with you, while others will help you plan your escape (take that however you want to). It doesn't matter if they are bigger, smaller, shorter, taller, richer or going through emotional turmoil all the time. You do not have to mix your sisterhood, either. Maintain the individuality and equality of each and every sisterhood relationships. It will quash any ill feelings you may begin to have by feeling that you are on the wrong side of a lopsided friendships.

 My 'R' is the woman I hope God disciplines me to be. He has found favor with her and she has found solace in His loving arms. Living right does not mean becoming a carbon copy of any other person. What God wants for you may not be what he wants for your sister girl, but that does not mean your gift from God is any less meaningful. My 'R' has shown me that God will meet you where YOU are and bring you to where He needs you to be. You may occasionally be there by yourself, but you are not alone. God will bring your sister girl to your side and show you His love through her eyes.

Your spiritual friend is _____
____ . Her light illuminates your dark days when she _____
_____ .

My 'T' sister is my cousin. Not related by blood, but as close to me as anyone could hope for. We went to the same schools. We played on the same softball team. We knew most of the same people growing up and we are each other's children's Godmother. Different events caused us to grow away from each other, but never truly apart. Even after years of separation, we are now back in each other's lives full force and I love her dearly. I realize that I don't have to talk to her every day to feel her love and know how close, admired, respected we are to each other. Our lives took us on two different paths, but my 'T' will forever be the number one sister in my hood.

Your life-long friend is _____ and we go back _____ years. (Hint: it must be at least 25 if you are old enough. You should have at least one lifelong friend.)

Now everything is not always smiles and giggles in your sisterhood. Take my other 'T' sister. When I met her I was under the impression this was going to be a lifelong bond. Co-workers at the same company, on the same level and with similar interests, I thought I would be able to include this sister for a lifetime. When I was in need, she stepped up and helped me at a very difficult time and, because I didn't want to jeopardize this friendship, I repaid it immediately and made a mental note not to ever hurt my friendships like that again. We partied regularly, but little did I know that there was a line being drawn in the sand that I was not aware of, nor was I aware that crossing it was seen as backstabbing in her eyes. This apparent sisterhood violation came when I accepted my promotion. All of a sudden I was the enemy and nothing I did was right. I heard complaints about my clothes, my hair and my overall lifestyle. I wasn't actually accused of trying to sleep with her husband, but the connotation came out in a conversation I was made privy to through the grapevine. Soon I was barred from her home and the friendship ended. Looking back on the whole mess, I finally pieced together when the breakdown occurred. I found out she had applied for the same position, but in a different office, and didn't get it. She transferred to another location and we lost touch. It was for the better, or so I thought. After a few years and office closings, guess who was back in the same building with me (smile). It has been a few years now and we still see each other on occasion in the halls or parking lot. We speak and remain cordial to one another, but that was a bond that was severed needlessly. I can't say I miss it, but it is what it is.

You bond was broken with _____ . I will leave it up to you if you choose to try to mend that fence or not. Not every sisterhood relationship should be saved.

 My 'V' girl is my blood sister. Through the years, we have had our ups and downs like any other siblings, but I can't imagine God giving us a better gift. We shared triumphs through adversity and we've mourned loss. I can call her 24/7 and know I will hear a warm "Hey Sis. Wassup?" It seems that we have become the cornerstone of the family and are the ones counted on to step up and take the reigns on any given matter. We were the first in our family to attend college. She is still a

light by which I gauge my successes. Not because I compete with her, but because I value her opinion on domestic and financial matters. She is a wealth of information, even when she doesn't know it. We laugh at the same movies, even if there are weeks in between the time we see it. We don't share the same taste in clothes or shoes, but that's ok, too. We do share a very important characteristic. Our mother's zest for life has been instilled in both of us

Your close sister is _____
and my parent(s) have blessed me with the perfect friend.

 My 'Y' sister is my former boss. Man oh Man. Let me tell you about a sister that is on the fast track to success. I am sure when you look in the dictionary you will see her picture next to any and maybe all of the following words. FAIR, STERN, COMPASSIONATE, HONEST, TRUSTED, and FUNNY. She is the boss you want to hate at times, but you can't help but know that she has your best interest at heart, even when she is in the middle of disciplining you. She will have your back in every situation publically, but will pull your coat and dress you down privately when you deserve it. Once she has been your boss, she will always be your boss, even if neither of you are in the same department or company. The only words I can use to describe her is *A MENTOR EXTRODINAIRE*.

Your (ex) boss friend is _____
__ and you are further in your career because she taught you to _____
_____.

Conclusion

Your network is not built on the number of sisters you have but in the quality and strength of the sisterhood relationships you maintain. As you fill in the blanks, look back at your give-and-take with your sister girls. You may even want to take a moment to call them and just say thank you for all they have enriched your life with. I encourage you to consider how important you are to them. Don't ever minimize your own self-worth to others in your hood. Sisterhood is an ever increasing circle. Much like a balloon, it contracts and expands in accordance with the substance you put into it.

ABOUT THE AUTHOR

ALICIA D. WHITE, MBA

The JordanMiles Group was birthed by Alicia D. White, MBA in August 2007 and the inspiration came from her two children Jourdyn and Myles. *TJMG* was founded after a failed marriage and years of wasting time and energy on unhealthy relationships. Our mission is to encourage, enlighten, & empower women and youth to learn to love themselves first in order to be able to effectively love someone else. Alicia is passionate about encouraging women to better their lives and the lives of their children. She believes that when given the right tools, women can overcome destructive behavior patterns and become better prepared for the right mate. She teaches character development, positive self – image, and self esteem and empowerment. She is also the local coordinator for Project Single Moms - Charlotte.

Alicia received her education from McKendree University, University of Louisville and Strayer University. Her background and training is in Human Resource Management and she has been blessed to travel extensively across the United States and work with Fortune 50 companies in executive HRM & Training roles. She is also certified through The Professional Woman Network in Women's Issues, Diversity, and Save Our Youth. Ms. White holds memberships in other professional organizations including The Urban League of the Central Carolinas - Young Professionals, The Professional Woman Network, The National Council of Negro Women (NCNW), National Black MBA Association, McKendree College Alumnae Association, Society of Human Resource Management (SHRM), Strayer University Alumnae Association and Project Single Moms. She is an active member of New Beginnings Community Church in Matthews, NC.

Alicia is available to present seminars and workshops to schools, churches, organizations, and individuals on a local and national basis.

Contact:
Alicia D. White, MBA
Founder
PO Box 3133
Matthews, NC 28106
adwhite@thejordanmilesgroup.com
www.thejordanmilesgroup.com

FIVE

HOW TO AVOID TOXIC RELATIONSHIPS:

STAYING AWAY FROM THE MARRIED MAN

By Alicia D. White, MBA

I remember like it was yesterday when I had my first encounter with a married man. I was a working high school senior. And I caught his eye one night while closing the store. He walked up behind and whispered sensuous words into my ear and it was on from there! I enjoyed going to work every day, even on Saturday and Sundays, if necessary. Something would go through me when he walked through the door. He told me that he was married, but I guess it just didn't matter enough to me to walk away. Here I was a senior in high school pulling a 30 year man. One of the bookkeepers must have noticed the eye contact that was being made between us and she called me into the break room and made me aware of her observation. That was my out, but I didn't take it!

A few years later I met Lanier. He walked up to me and placed the most passionate kiss on me that I had ever experienced. He was so handsome and debonair and everything I thought I wanted in a mate. We had met online on Blackplanet, I think in March of that year. We chatted for almost four months before we decided to meet up in Atlanta the weekend of July 4th. The mini-vacation was unforgettable and leaving was the last thing I wanted to. When we returned back to our home state the following Tuesday, he went one way and I went another, certain that it was the beginning of a promising future! Why did I think that? What made me so sure that he was the one? I didn't have a contact number for him. All I had was an email address and I knew the location of his job that brought him to my city, but I didn't know the EXACT address. I found myself waiting for him to call or stop by or even send me an email. Deep down, I knew what was going on, but I compromised my intuition for what I was feeling at that moment. Eventually he called from a "friends" number and the call lasted maybe fifteen minutes. But that few minutes held me over for the next week or so when he found time to call me again from the "friends" number.

Friends kept telling me that he was either involved with someone or he was married, but I refused to accept that the man that I had just fallen for would lie to me about something so important. So I continued to see him when he could make time for me. On the outside I was okay with the every now and then, but on the inside it was killing me softly. I was selling myself short, but too far gone to recognize and acknowledge it. Eventually, after a little detective work, it was confirmed that he was, in fact, married. I allowed him to give me his excuses, I went off, I cried, and I still continued to see him. This went on for months that led to years, three years to be exact.

Then there was Randall, a successful salesman with a smile that would light up a room! I met him while working for a Fortune 500 company. He was very up front and honest with me about his situation, but that didn't stop him from pursuing a romantic relationship with me. It was exciting and spontaneous, but still very lonely. I saw him when it was convenient FOR HIM (do we see a pattern?), so that made me an option, but in my eyes he was a priority. I made changes to my schedule to accommodate his because he had to be home at a decent time (before she got home). The sex was amazing, but it was only temporary, as it lasted maybe an hour, or if I was lucky, two. But I never saw him on the weekends and you can just forget about holidays and birthdays, since they always came a week after the actual birth date. Kind of took the fun out of celebrating another year of birth. This went on for almost a year; then I decided I wanted something more, something of my own. By no means do I fault my lovers, because I was a willing participant, I knew better, and I could have easily said enough is enough and walked away. But I didn't.

For better or worse, some women seem to always be attracted to married men. I was one of those women. And if you're this type of woman, it may be somewhat frustrating or confusing for you. When you think about it though, it does make some sense. Married men put off a stability vibe. And in today's modern day world, stability is important, yet rare. But even with this type of stability comes consequences.

Are you willing to deal with the consequences of being involved with a married man? Why?

(Your answer goes on the line provided.)

The problem with dating a married man when you are single is that you remain single throughout the affair. As much as we would like to be a couple, you are not a couple, so don't fool yourself. Sure, you may act like a couple when you are together, but in reality you aren't. In the very beginning you will see quite a lot of him, especially during working hours. Secret dates will be established and the excitement will make you feel alive. But as soon as the guilt sets in, excuses will develop and you will be kept hanging on, but you'll be forever available just in case he can work out an escape for a few hours. It is a subtle process and by the time you realize it, it's often too late to save your heart.

You will never be without a phone on the off chance that he will call. He wants to see you, but you must be understanding of his situation because it's not easy for him to get away. And because you so understand, you will receive the highest of accolades that will probably come with jewelry, gifts and/or money. You have just become a saint and a martyr and the best thing since sliced white bread. In the meantime (while you're at home with your diamond tennis bracelet, STILL alone), he will be at home with his wife and children (possibly) living life as a family while you're wondering when you will see him again. You will have to endure endless months of discussing what it will be like when you are together (which you probably never will) and you will face comparisons with their spouse at every turn, even if he never vocalizes it.

You will be expected to be available, just in case, because one can never tell when your crutch-like strength will be required, and you will be thankful for any small minute of time you are given. They will insist that the evening you had a week last Thursday was a great deal for them to arrange so be grateful and that you should just hang on for them if you love them. And so it goes on, month after month. Of course, the key thing that makes your affair different from everyone else's is that it is 'different'. Your passion and love is almost unique and you know they are in a terrible marriage, they made a mistake, and you will be perfect together. In other words, you will make excuses whenever possible to justify the situation – just a little more time and things will be fantastic.

No one else (not even your girlfriends) can possibly understand what you both are going through and so you will withdraw from some of your friends, partly because you think they strongly disapprove of what you are doing. In actuality, they do understand and probably have been in your situation a time or two. Your weekends will be wasted, as will vacations because whilst you are alone waiting at home for the phone to ring, they will be at social functions and parties and all kinds of domestic events that you would die to have, but are never afforded the opportunity of having. You trust your lover completely. After all, you are in this together. The thing is, your entire relationship is already founded on deceit and lies. And if they can do it to their husband or wives, they can also do it to you. And that will happen. Eventually!

If your lover was going to leave his wife, he would have to leave for them and not for you. If they are going to do it for themselves, it will be much sooner rather than later. If they haven't become single within three to four months, they probably never will. They must leave not for you, but for their own reasons. If he leaves for you, you will be held silently accountable every time life is not perfect. And for all you know, they may always be looking backwards with a half-glance and all that they left behind.

Walk away as fast as possible in the opposite direction and keep walking. Never fool yourself; dating a married man is a complete waste of time in 99% of cases. A very few do make it through, but almost all don't. You will have absolutely no idea as to what he is going through and you will be nothing more than light relief to something far more serious.

You will lose self-respect because you are sharing your lover, you are falling in love with someone you cannot have, you are second best most of the time and you will be extremely lonely. Most of the evenings will not be with your loved one, so your relationship cannot grow, and much of what you do will be based around sex, not love. Your relationship will be extremely intense, but will be sporadic and unfulfilling. As a woman, you will be made to feel cheap and may even fall pregnant, in which case your situation has just become highly complex.

The thing I cannot stress enough is how much you will be lied to. The person you love will be telling you lies almost constantly. It is not that he is essentially a bad person, but over time he gets used to lying to spare feelings while protecting himself and his marriage. Please remember that in the midst of such emotional turmoil, he will have no option but to consider himself. In the end, he will find lying to everyone second nature, even though it may be cutting him up emotionally. A married lover simply wants to sit on the fence and never make a decision. They want you to decide for them, which of course you cannot. You could demand that he leave his wife for you once and for all, but in doing so, you are now standing in the firing line.

Do you really want a man that left his wife for you? Seriously, if he left her for you, what would stop him from leaving you for somebody else?

Do value yourself, understand yourself and if you truly believe that there are some truly great single people out there?

Why would you waste your life on dating a married person?

For all these words, people will continue to learn from their own mistakes and in doing so, pass on their valuable lessons to others. But for the sake of some short-term passionate sex, you truly could be risking everything. I pray for you strength and wisdom to walk away and not look back.

Most people have the desire for a happy, fulfilling relationship where both parties are mutually respectful, loving, and caring. When both partners have emotional balance and a level of commitment and effort, this result is certainly possible. However, there are instances in which one or both individuals bring personal issues into the relationship that cause hurt and destruction within the partnership. Whether it is addiction, abusive tendencies, unfaithfulness, or other damaging behaviors, the result can be a toxic situation for the other partner.

Here are just a few steps to avoid such a toxic relationship, whether you are just getting out of such a relationship, or seeking to avoid the potential for one in the future:

1.	Take care of yourself physically and send yourself the message that you are worthy of the effort and care. Your mental and physical well being is also tied together, so supporting the health of your body will help support a stable mental state. Start a doctor approved exercise program, ideally centered on cardiovascular exercise. This type of workout encourages the release of endorphins, feel good compounds that elevate mood.

2.	Surround yourself with people who are supportive, loving, and affirming. This is key because the actions and words of the toxic partner can be like programming, which causes you to assimilate and believe negative messages about yourself. Immersing yourself in more positive and affirming messages from your support system will help you deprogram the false beliefs about yourself and reality. Join a faith bible based church and build a relationship with the ultimate love, Jesus Christ. He'll never lead you the wrong way!

3.	Always pay attention to your instincts and red flag warnings. Women's intuition is real – DO NOT IGNORE IT!! Sometimes when we are in a toxic relationship, we learn to push aside and ignore the warning bells that are going off all the time to warn us of impending physical, emotional, and spiritual danger. It is important to begin to reactivate our awareness of these instincts. Start with noting in your body how you feel around certain people and situations. Are you relaxed, peaceful, and safe? Or are you agitated, anxious, or ashamed around others? This may be telling you what you need to do and who you should move toward or away from.

4.	Avoid contact with your ex, and/or other people that your instincts tell you might be toxic. Your toxic ex partner will likely employ the same tactics which have worked on you to this point to either draw you back into the relationship, or at least maintain some control. You need time and space to heal and reprogram the negative messages that came from the actions and words of your toxic ex partner.

For someone in a toxic relationship, or with a history of being involved in toxic relationships, breaking away is often very difficult. If you've gotten involved and attached to someone who struggles with damaging personal issues – addiction, abusive tendencies, and cheating behavior, just to name a few – the result is often a lowered sense of self-worth, feelings of incapability or inferiority, or even doubts about his or her own perceptions of reality. This can make the prospects of going it alone seem overwhelming, and there may be that voice in the back of your head that wonders if you really deserve this treatment.

Signs that you are in a toxic relationship:

1. You know he's married and still choose to be in a relationship. (That's an obvious sign.)

2. You feel isolated from family and friends.

3. If you cannot trust your partner and believe in their word, then there really is no future together.

4. Your partner criticizes, belittles, or does not defend you in front of or to family members, friends or even strangers.

5. Your partner may also neglect you, disappear from time to time without any care for your feelings, and blame you for their cheating, negative behavior, and failures.

As you evaluate your current relationship and one of these applies to you – run run as fast as you can!!

The mind, body and soul are the three key elements that allow healthy adult relationships to flourish. We fall into toxic relationships when we allow one element to be the primary force in our decision making when seeking a mate and we tend to push the other two to the backburner. In order to be fulfilled, we must enter into a relationship as a whole person; when you seek a person to complete you, that is when you run into problems. Often, we carry our own toxic baggage from our childhood or past relationships with us for so long that we allow it to define who we are. When we allow the past to define us, we fall into a victim's mentality. It develops self-esteem issues and creates an emotional barrier that no one can get through. As you find balance within your own mind, body and soul, you will attract those who have the same sense of inner peace. This is the best way to avoid toxic romantic relationships.

What is it that you want for your life?

1. _____

2. _____

3. _____

4. _____

5. _____

What is holding you back from making the best choices to achieve the life you deserve?

1. _____

2. _____

3. _____

4. _____

5. _____

When you get to the point that you are sick and tired of being sick and tired and you take the first step to get out of your toxic relationship, you'll be somewhat sad and may be scared, but keep going. You can do it!! When you feel like turning back – PLEASE DON'T! Take a deep breath, repeat the serenity prayer several times and take the next step!

"God grant me the serenity to accept the things I cannot change, the courage to change the things I can, and the wisdom to know the difference."

If I can do it – you can too!!

ABOUT THE AUTHOR

STACY L. HENDERSON, PhD

Stacy L. Henderson, PhD, is the Founder and President of Dr. Stacy L. Henderson & Associates, a firm which specializes in personal and professional development through coaching, consulting and training. She conducts seminars and workshops that have been presented nationwide and abroad. Her training topics include: Self-Esteem and Empowerment, Women as Leaders, Enhancing Your Professional Image, Dealing with Change & Transition and Teen Etiquette to name a few. Dr. Henderson has been trained and certified by the Professional Woman Network (PWN). She is a Certified Professional Coach, Certified Youth Trainer and is internationally recognized a Certified Diversity Trainer, specializing in Women's Issues. She is a contributing author for the following books in the PWN African-American Library: Wellness for the African-American Woman: Mind, Body and Spirit; Raising African-American Boys; Raising African-American Girls; and The Woman's Handbook for Self-Confidence - which are available nationally and in the Caribbean.

Dr. Henderson has a Bachelor of Science in Education, with a Specialization in Workforce Education and Development; a Master of Arts in Health Services Management; and Doctorates in Business Administration and Christian Leadership. She is a member of the Professional Woman Network (PWN), the National Association of Female Executives (NAFE), the American College of Health Care Executives (ACHE), Delta Sigma Theta Sorority, Inc., and National Naval Officers' Association.

Dr. Henderson is dedicated to motivating individuals to achieve their best mental, physical and spiritual health. She is available to consult on a local, national and international basis. She is available for individual and group coaching and consulting sessions, religious functions, military events, youth assemblies, seminars and conferences.

Contact:
Dr. Stacy L. Henderson & Associates
Personal & Professional Coaching and Consulting
P. O. Box 886913
Great Lakes, Illinois 60088-6913
Email: SLHenderson007@aol.com
www.protrain.net

SIX

WHEN GOD TURNED MY LIFE AROUND

By Dr. Stacy Henderson

Introduction

I received Christ in my life at an early age. I have always been very inquisitive and there were oftentimes thoughts and notions running around inside my head like, why is the sky blue and how do we really know what color blue is supposed to be? How can the sky be the limit when there are footprints on the moon? Is the Earth round or flat? When we reach the end of the Earth, do we fall off the edge or roll over the side? I have also wondered, who am I and where do I fit in the big scheme of things?

Reflections

Now that I think back on it, it seems silly, but I remember asking countless questions like these. I loved to read so I was an avid reader and a great speller. After reading what seemed like hundreds of books and sharing my notions with my mother, sometimes she would laugh and other times she looked at me in wonder. Then one day, she sat me down and taught me how to read the Bible and search the scriptures for guidance, wisdom and understanding. She was always reading books and singing. Those are things that I love to do most – probably because of her. At an early age, I developed a great love for reading and writing.

I was a tall, thin, lanky girl in my youth. I was a nerd, or so I was called. The popular kids at school always seemed to have the best clothes and extra money to spend. I figured out a way to be a member of that crowd. I asked for the clothes they wore and changed my hairstyle to look like theirs did. I did not wear my glasses as much because I needed to look less like a nerd. But in addition to finally fitting in – I was smart. I could answer the questions the teachers were going to ask before they could even ask it. How? I was a good reader and an awesome speller and I liked sharing what I learned with others. Yes, I know. I was acting like a nerd.

I was determined to dispel that myth about me so I decided that if I acted tough, others would think I was tough. I hung around school with my cliché and we had a lot of fun together. We cut classes. We shoplifted candy and gum from the local store and we got into trouble a lot in school. All the while we were having fun, I did not realize the impact our actions would have on our lives. Sure we were children, but even children grow up someday, don't they?

In elementary school I was the teacher's pet although I was quiet and shy. I also had a certain group of friends that made me a part of the group and considered me 'one of them' – or so I thought. I recall many trips to the principal's office, where my mother would get a call because I was acting out or had not been to class. Those were the days when teachers had your parents' permission to paddle the students. Needless to say, I was paddled in school and again once my mother got home from work. Of course, she had to find me first; I usually hid in a closet or under a bed. I remember those days like they were yesterday. In my home, my father came home from work long after my mother had gotten home. So she was the parent who mainly ran the household and dished out the punishment. She was very good at it.

Lessons Learned

Back then, it did not matter to me so much to me that I ran with a 'bad element', as I often heard my friends referred to. I fit in, I was part of the group and they liked me.

One day while I was in my bedroom alone after being grounded for an incident (which was not my fault) I had an epiphany: I was tired of always being in trouble and getting grounded. Earlier that day someone had set fire to all of the toilet paper rolls in the girl's bathroom. It was one of my friends and I knew who did it, but I refused to tell on her. Another student said that I was the fire starter. I was not. However, I was the one who provided my friend that started the fire with the book of matches. How foolish was that?

That same evening, shortly after getting my usual spanking, the telephone rang. It was one of my friends I had gotten into trouble with in school earlier that day. My mother called me to the telephone. Now, my mother was no-nonsense and I knew she meant business. She stood there staring at me with a look on her face that clearly said, "Stacy, you are grounded. I dare you to take this receiver." And although she spoke no words, the message was loud and clear. I simply asked my mother to tell whoever it was that I could not have calls until after I was no longer grounded. She relayed the message and hung up the telephone. I realized at that moment that I was often disciplined for getting into some kind of trouble. And believe me, my mother was good at dishing out the punishment. Ironically, the group of friends I was with seemed to either get off easy or have no punishment at all. From time to time I was sent to the principal's office for being the class clown or telling silly jokes to make the other students laugh. Of course, I loved school so I finished my assignments early, then I would entertain my classmates. My mother believed in education so I knew that if I did not get good grades, she would surely send me to the all-girls private school. From time to time she would gently remind me that that was an option if I could not get it together in the public school I attended.

My mother also used to tell me that one day I would get my 'come-uppance,' whatever that meant. That cycle of 'mischievousness' as she called it would be broken, but it would probably take something serious for that to happen. Of course, something did. I distinctly recall shoplifting with a childhood friend at a local supermarket. We were both stealing, just as we had many times before. As we were leaving, security grabbed us both, took us into the back of the store and called our parents. My friend's mother came to the store and took her home. Mine never came. I told the officer she was probably just tired from working and asked that he drive me home, since I lived about three blocks away. As the police officer was driving me home, we saw my mother walking down the street toward the store where I was caught stealing. I asked the officer to pull over, which he did. The officer spoke with my mother and all I could hear her say was, "Take her to the local children's center. I'll pick her up sooner or later." I thought she was only kidding, so I shrugged my shoulders and laughed. Needless to say, the joke was on me as I watched her (through the rear window of the squad car) as she stood there with both hands on her hips and watched the car drive away. As the tears rolled down my cheeks, I realized that this was different than any other punishment. Normally, I was withheld privileges or spanked. This time, I would be taken away from all that was familiar to me, family and home. Clearly, my mother was fed up with my antics.

Going Through

After I was taken to the local children's center, I settled in reluctantly, because I did not want to be there. There were too many children – all of them strangers, and more rules than I care to remember. I simply wanted to go home. After a few hours passed and my mother had not come for me, I decided to make the most of it, even though I had no idea how long I would be there. Well, I found myself there a few weeks later; I even spent my next birthday there. At the time I thought it was cruel of my mother to allow this to happen to me.

All of the children there all had a story to tell. Some were abandoned. Some were abused and/or neglected. Some had run away from home for one reason or another. Others were, as some of the staff called us, 'trouble makers' – when they thought we were not listening. I was none of those things. I got good grades and I was a great speller. Besides that, I could beat anybody at all things academic because I was very studious. Now, with all of that going for me, I kept asking myself, "How did I end up in here?" Then one day it hit me: this was the serious thing my mother had spoken about. This was my "come-uppance." That moment, I decided to do something different. I needed a change. Not being able to talk with my friends on the telephone was one thing, but being taken away in a police car and placed in a children's center was totally different.

Turning Point

Once my mother sent for me, I found it difficult to face her when I got home. And when she and I talked about it, she simply said, "You did it to yourself." She talked about how all of my actions had consequences. She said that I had a mind of my own and I needed to use it, not allow others to think for me. She said I was smart and she expected better because I had been taught better. Then, she said she was disappointed in my behavior. Those words hurt me because I knew right then and there that I had hurt her. I was disappointed in myself and I knew I had to change.

She was right. I did know better and I decided that I wanted to not only do better, but to be better. I did not bother to tell her that I just wanted to fit in with my group of friends because I was tired of being teased about my looks, or called a nerd because I was a good student. Knowing my mother like I did, she would probably ask something like, "If they asked you to jump off a bridge, would you jump?" Parents are smart that way.

One night I was in our house and I could hear my mother reading the book of Job from her Bible. She often read aloud and this particular night I knew she was still upset with me so I sat outside the door and listened. Later, I eased into her bedroom and asked her who he was and why she was so interested in him. She read me the story, then shared some insight on how he was blessed, basically stripped of all God had given him, and then blessed even more abundantly because of his faith that God would restore him. She said Job had great patience, something she needed to deal with me. We laughed until we cried. I knew I was a handful but I was struggling with childhood issues. Issues I just did not think she would understand. So I kept them to myself… for the moment.

That same night, out of nowhere, I started writing things down. We always had to have spiral bound notebooks for school, so I used one to write about that experience and what I learned from it. Like my mother said, there is a blessing in every life lesson.

As time passed, I began to keep track of the things I wanted to do with my life: Learn more about God, not have my mother be disappointed in me, love myself more, have a family of my own, travel the world, join the military because my father was a Marine and he had such great adventures, and sing my heart out because I loved music. Back then life seemed so simple and I did not really need much since my parents took care of everything anyway.

The spiral notebooks were the foundation for what we called keeping a diary. Today we call it journaling. In mine I created fantasies of living in far away lands and of having a lot of leisure time for playing in the park, being a princess or swimming in the ocean with dolphins. I loved dolphins. Mind you – I was afraid of water and rarely even went to the community swimming pool. So I must have had some imagination back then. But it was always fun to dream.

Every now and then I remembered that story about Job. I knew what it meant to believe in God, but I did not quite comprehend faith. The word itself sounded strong, yet I did not fully understand its true meaning. I asked my mother to explain it because she always seemed to have the answers to the questions I often asked. She always had a story to tell or some anecdote to help me deal with life in general. She was able to show me things that were right in front of me that I was unable to see. She had something called 'wisdom.'

I began reading the Bible stories almost every day. I wrote down the meaning of a lot of the parables and the morals of the stories. My spiral notebooks were piling up and I was good at remembering lessons and the meaning of scriptures and words. They helped me to understand life better.

Purpose

My mother and I read many Bible stories together and she taught me how to pray and talk to God daily. She taught me how to trust in Him and to seek Him. Again, I was a young child, but for some reason she felt strongly that I needed those lessons at that time. She would often tell me that God was preparing her to prepare me for the life I was destined to live. She said He had a purpose for me and that I had a special calling. That was a foreign concept to me, but I knew that if my mother said it, it must have been true. She explained that trials and tribulations would come my way and that I needed faith that God would get me through them – no matter what they were. Life is not always fair and it would not be easy living. She also said that I needed to always remember that no matter what obstacles the world put in my way, God would always make a way for me to get around them. Nothing was impossible with God.

Changed

I went to church often and eventually joined the children's choir. I loved to sing because my mother loved singing. She was always singing some hymn or humming a tune if she did not remember the words. Melodies seemed to lift her spirits as she lifted up Zion with her voice. I loved that about her. At my church, Little Bryan Missionary Baptist

Church, we always put on Christian plays, musicals and programs where the young people could perform. I loved to write so I often shared my poems. I had a deep understanding of words and their meanings so it was easy for me to express myself in that way. I loved acting in the plays because I got to 'be' some of the characters I wrote about and read about. In Christ, I was transformed and it was wonderful.

As I progressed into adolescence, many of the things my mother shared with me came to pass. I struggled with peer pressure, abuse, insecurities and doubts about myself. It took time for me to understand how loved and how truly blessed I was. As a child I often heard it from my parents, but as I developed my own sense of knowing, I discovered that I was in control of my destiny. I was responsible for my own actions and would be held accountable for them.

Conclusion

Had my mother not introduced me to Christ, I do not know where I would be today. I have often wondered if I would have continued along that path of getting into trouble and perhaps, would have ended up a menace to society. Would I have survived this long had I not decided to make positive changes in my life? What if I had not had a mother who, in spite of my misdeeds, loved me unconditionally?

I barely kept in touch with my childhood friends after my 'come-uppance.' By the time I was ready to graduate high school, I had moved to the other side of town and had lost touch with many of them. We simply drifted apart. Every now and then, I would see a news story on television or read a newspaper article noting that one of them had fallen victim to one or more of the tragedies of life: drugs, promiscuity, crime, street violence. I suppose that sooner or later we all get our 'come-uppance.'

Today, everyone has grown up and life continues. I hear from a few of those old friends periodically but we have long-distance friendships. Although we may have been misfits in our youth, many of us are still here – surviving. Some are doctors, lawyers, teachers, servicemen, servicewomen, and positive role models. Not everyone had a bad ending. And even though some are no longer with us and I do not know the fate of some of the others, I keep them and their loved ones in prayer. There are no harsh feelings between us because we were young back then and we were carefree. We did not know how much potential we had.

As I sit here as a woman, and at the age I am, I realize that the little girl I was back then longed to be accepted and she wanted to be loved. The wonderful thing is.....she always was – even before she ever *truly* knew it.

In Loving Memory of my mother, Mary E. Scott Henderson

Notes:

_____

_____

_____

_____

_____

_____

_____

_____

_____

_____

_____

_____

_____

_____

_____

_____

_____

_____

_____

_____

ABOUT THE AUTHOR

TAKENIA CANADY

Takenia Canady is a professional accountant in the Raleigh/Durham, NC Area. She was born in the small town of Sanford, NC. Takenia attended North Carolina State University where she received her Bachelor degree in Accounting. She is a loving wife and mother. Takenia enjoys reading, beach trips, and spending time with her family. Against all odds of parental and domestic abuse she is living her dream of helping young women.

Contact:
takenia_r@hotmail.com

SEVEN

SURVIVING THE ABUSE

By Takenia Canady

We are taught as children that "Sticks and stones may break my bones, but words will never hurt me." Someone should have added in an exception that stated, "Unless these words are coming from your mother." Hurtful words coming from your mother can kill. Emotional abuse is often minimized, yet it can leave deep and lasting scars. They assault your self-esteem, curse your future, and stamp a lethal label on your life.

"You are never going to amount to anything." These are the harsh words I remember so clearly coming from a doped up mother. How does a child handle such hurtful words, you may ask? I used the negativity as ammunition to push me to a better future. I was determined to prove my mother wrong. I persevered through all the name calling, fights, and disturbed sleep.

I was reared by my maternal grandmother and great-grandmother. Both of them tried to keep me sheltered from my mother's drug addiction, but as I got older, things became very clear.

The average teenage girl comes home from school to do homework, chats with friends over the phone, enjoys the latest BET television and retires to bed. I, on the other hand had to constantly prepare myself for a doped mother. She was constantly stealing my personal items. I was awakened late at night by collect calls from the Lee County Jail as my mother was arrested on a very regular basis. It was difficult for me to have phone conversations due to the unruly appearances by my mother. I remember one incident very clearly. "Let me use the phone, Kena," says my mother as she slurs her words because of the alcohol. At the time, I was not the most respectful daughter because I lost all respect for my mother over the years. I responded with attitude. "Wait, I am about to hang up." Then she came lunging after me saying, "Bitch, give me the phone." This ended in the phone getting slammed to the floor and my mother and I having an all-out fight. I remember thinking to myself, a fight with the woman who is supposed to nurture me and protect me from harm? How could this be happening to me?

At the time, I could not see how this abusive relationship would lead me to another abusive relationship, but it did. I am living proof that individuals who were verbally abused by a parent find themselves in similar situations as an adult. My similar situation began when I met…let's just call him Justin for the purpose of this book. Now Justin was as fine as wine. He was the guy that every woman wanted and he chose me. I remember when I laid eyes on him at the Apple Chill in Chapel Hill, NC. He approached me and let me know how beautiful I was. My heart almost melted. Even then I never thought we would end up in a relationship, but we did. Things were going great in the beginning. We talked on the phone for hours and hours. He was such a gentleman. We went to the movies, enjoyed candlelight dinners and shopping. The relationship moved pretty fast. After our first date I was moving my things from my grandmother's house into his house at the age of nineteen. Justin stated, "My woman should be living with me!" I should have noticed this need to have control, but I was too young and in love. Justin was twenty-four, so my grandmother totally disagreed with the situation. However, there was no stopping me. Little did I know this was only an optical illusion.

Our living arrangement was smooth sailing the first month, but after awhile Justin did not want me to hang out with my friends any longer. He only wanted me to go to school and come back home. He even had a problem with me having phone conversations. Justin had begun to be over- controlling and he was isolating me away from everyone. (Ladies, please realize these are clear signs of a potential physical abuser.) I didn't realize it because I could not see past the love I had for Justin.

Our first argument was when the physical abuse began. I had moved out of Justin's place and was living back with my grandmother. One night after I came home from work, I got a call from Justin. He told me how much he missed me and loved me. He wanted to come by and see me and I agreed. When he arrived, we talked and hugged. He convinced me to come with him to his house. I was so ecstatic that we were going to work things out.

As we began getting closer to his house, I noticed his tone was changing from loving and sincere to very stern and hateful. He screamed out at me, "You are MY woman. Do you know who I am? I am Justin French!!" I could not figure out where his anger was coming from. When we made it into the house, he picked up a beer can and threw it against the wall. I was so scared. Then he grabbed me and began to choke me. I remember thinking, "Oh God, he is going to kill me!" Justin must have read my mind because he yelled out, "I should kill you bitch!" I closed my eyes and thought to myself, "How did I end up here?" **One in four**

women (25%) has experienced domestic violence in her lifetime, according to The Centers for Disease Control and Prevention.

After Justin decided I had been choked long enough, he instantly began to apologize and tell me how much he loved me. He began to act as if I was not just gasping for breath. Unfortunately, the relationship did not end here. I accepted all of Justin's apologies. I convinced myself that he only hit me because he loved me. As time went on, my weight began to decrease drastically and my friends began to worry about me. I remember seeing my best friend in the grocery store and her eyes were filled with concern. She called out my name and I looked to Justin for permission to go and speak to her. You see, after the first abusive episodes and several other episodes that followed, I became very afraid of Justin; I felt like I had to walk on eggshells around him. I always watched what I said and did in order to avoid a blow up.

My friend said to me, "Girl, what is going on? You are so small. Your clothes are hanging off of you and your hair is bigger than your head." I just laughed it off and said that Justin liked for his women to be small. We hugged and went our separate ways. My friend knew in her heart something wasn't right. **Nearly three out of four (74%) Americans personally know someone who is or has been a victim of domestic violence, according to Allstate Foundation National Poll on Domestic Violence.**

Once I found Justin in the grocery store, he looked at me with anger in his eyes. He grabbed me by my arm and accused my friend of trying to hook me up with someone. He justified grabbing my arm by saying, "If you were not such a worthless whore getting hook ups, I would not have to act this way!" Again he apologized and again I accepted.

When we returned home he made me sit on the floor. Justin said to me, "Sit on the floor. You are dirty trash and you do not belong on my furniture. You are worthless and no one else will want you." He had me right where he wanted me. He was keeping me from my family and friends. In order to decrease my dependence on him, he had cut me off from the outside world. I had to ask permission to go anywhere, do anything, or see anyone.

Our break up cycle continued for months. We broke up, I moved out and in with my grandmother. He apologized and I took him back. During one of our off seasons, I decided to go out with my girls to the club. We were having a blast. The DJ played every song we wanted to hear. The night could not get any better. I came home only to find Justin waiting for me in the driveway. He approached me with that charming smile. I was weak as usual and I gave in. I hopped into the car with him. He began to tell me how beautiful I looked and then all of sudden he snapped. Out of nowhere his fist connected with my head. He punched me in my temple over and over again. I tried to open the car door and jump out. I was determined he was going to kill me. He pressed his foot to the gas, drove with one hand, and punched me with the other. When we drove up to his house, he pulled me from the passenger side to the driver's side and threw me into the dirt. Justin began to throw the dirt at me and told me I was never going to amount to anything. He tried to make me eat the dirt from the ground. He dragged me into the front door and down the hallway. Once again I began to ask why? What did I do? Why was this happening to me? I begged for him to just leave me alone but he still wasn't finished with me. Justin took two of his fingers and rammed them down my throat. I knew this was the end for me. This went on for about five minutes. But to me, it felt like hours. Finally, he released me and I ran into the guest bedroom. There was so much blood on my shirt and my throat was in so much pain. I finally drifted off to sleep. Then I was awakened by Justin tearing my shorts off and climbing on top of me. He covered my mouth so I could not scream and he proceeded to rape me. Once he reached his climax, he returned to his room. I washed up and retired to bed.

Of course, the following day was filled with apologies, but I'd had enough. Blessings and curses should not come from the same mouth. I packed up my clothes and moved back in with my grandmother and this time for good. Justin called and called but I would not take any of his phone calls.

One cold wintery night I decided to write my grandmother a letter because I had let her down so much. It went something like this:

Dear Mom,

I know that I have disappointed you time and time again, but I promise I will make it up to you. I will make you proud of me again. I have enrolled in school and I am moving forward with my life in a positive direction. Please forgive me for all the pain I have caused. Thank you for the long nights of praying. I love you!!
Kena.

The night I reconciled with my grandmother was also the last night I would hear Justin's voice. I received a phone call around 2 am from a very close friend. Justin had been shot. I was picked up by a family member and taken to the hospital. When I arrived he was already dead. My body was so numb. So many thoughts ran through my head. It's amazing how the person that treated me so badly could still have such a huge piece of my heart. I cried and cried. I couldn't believe he was gone. When I saw him being placed into the ground, I made a promise to myself that he would be the last person to physically harm me.

Although the next few months were very hard for me, I continued to press on. I was determined not to allow my circumstances to determine my situation. I finished the two year program at community school and obtained my associates in arts/pre-English degree. I was accepted to North Carolina State University, where I received my Bachelor's in accounting. I met a wonderful man whom I later married and his main goal is to put a smile on my face. When I think about MY STORY, I can't help but give GOD GLORY!

My career and family life is going great. The trials I have been through helped me to become the person I am today. It is very important to me that young women hear my story. If any of the readers are in a violent situation, please get out immediately. It only gets worse. DOMESTIC ABUSE IS REAL!!!

ABOUT THE AUTHOR

KIM ROBINSON

 Kim is President and Ceo of Girlfriends International, a women's outreach ministry designed for personal and professional development as well as spiritual growth. The ministry specializes in workshops, seminars, and training programs designed to educate, empower and speak words of life to women. Kim has developed teaching material that boldly confronts a wide variety of issues that women care deeply about. Her compassion for women and the issues they face is deep and abiding. Kim has overcome personal adversities that have made her an awesome motivational teacher with a passion to uplift the whole woman body, mind, and spirit.

Kim has extensive experience and a diverse background in the area of elderly care, mental health, severely handicapped, autism, and physical disablement, as well as self-sufficiency services. She acquired hands on knowledge by working with her family business, Serenity Village – ALF & Developmental Disabilities Services, that was founded in 2001 by her sister Tammy Hartfield who is deceased. Kim is an ordained Evangelist. A certified trainer in Women Issues; she is also a member of the Professional Women Network. Kim is co-author in PWN book of " Bruised But Not Broken" Kim is an advocate for the awareness of bipolar disorder. Kim is available for seminars, and workshops and women conferences, she is an exceptional keynote speaker.

I would like to dedicate this chapter to three wonderful women in my life. My mother Norma Hartfield and my aunt Alice Hennessy and my cousin Karen Hennessy who are strong independent Christian women who have prayed for me and continues to support me.

Contact:
Kim Robinson
1403 4th St SW
Largo, FL 33770
850-333-1724
Kimrobinson.sisterkeeper@gmail.com

EIGHT

I'M MY SISTERS KEEPER

By Kim Robinson

Keeper –" …but Ruth clave unto her." "And Ruth said, entreat me not to leave thee or to return from following after thee."—Ruth I, 14 and 16

I profoundly love and deeply respect my sisters, along with the grace of God and His anointing, I pledge to pursue my purpose with passion and integrity by teaching you only what He has put in my heart. —Kim

Sisters, in this chapter we will look at what it will take to complete and fulfill ourselves as women. My objective is to show you what a whole woman is and how you can become one. Hopefully, after reading this chapter, you will recognize her when you encounter her, and you will desire to be like her and have nothing missing and nothing broken. So, if you are ready, come take this journey with me to a place of peace and respect for yourself and other women.

To be a true sister's keeper I must always share the truth. I must set an example that all sisters will inspire to follow and it is imperative for me to give you information that will be life changing. On this life journey we have probably passed each other a number of times, not paying attention or showing affection or empathy for one another. We have been bruised and broken, left to tend to our own wounds of heartache and pain. We have been so desperate in our attempt to keep things hidden that the mask has become permanently attached to our face, and if we are not careful, we may be in danger of not becoming women who are whole.

I believe one of the best ways for us to learn and grow is through the experience of others. Therefore, I have placed **Sister-to-Sister** testaments throughout out the chapter. These are true statements from different women about the issues they face. We all have something to learn from each other. We can all show each other the way.

Souls of My Sisters

"You can never see the true person in front of you until you stop judging them."—Merna Throne

Let me begin by saying, I need you as you are the only one who understands what it is to be me, the true essence of myself, Woman. Through your eyes I see me and to be honest, it's not always a pretty picture. I'm not talking about outward beauty because we seem to have that in check. We use make-up, we get our hair and nails and pedicures done. We have spent a small fortune in time and money on these services. Believe me, I know you are worth it. But my concern is that, when you get home and remove the mask, no one is there to see the real you. Let's just face it sisters, you have deceived yourself and allowed others to do so to the point that you have no clue as to who you are. That's why you look for yourself in people, places and things that will never be able to reveal to you your true self. Trust me, I know.

Sister-to-Sister: I needed you, but I couldn't let you know. As we stood and socialized after church service, could you not see the loneliness in my eyes or the heartbreak of so many disappointments? Why didn't you ask me to join you and your friends for dinner? Was it because of your fear of me finding out who you truly are? But you walked off and left me to face your back. I often wonder, did you see my need?

It's Never Too late to Become What You Almost Were.

"Accept the difference to being different."

In 1995, I opened a consignment shop in my hometown. I called it "Women at Large," intended to be for plus size women. But God's plan was different; it was for ALL women. Daily as women came in, it began to turn into a testimony/prayer shop. It got to the point that if you came in to shop, you most likely would find me praying with a sister. I loved it. It was as natural as breathing. The great thing about being in business for me is that I could dedicate it to God. It actually was an unveiling of my ministry, but I did not recognize it then. Now that I know what my life purpose is, I have great passion to pursue it. If you are waiting for the Lord to speak and reveal purpose and destiny to you, I can almost guarantee that He has. By simply asking the question, we begin to get answers. The answers may not be what we want to hear, but they are necessary and they help us wake from our long-deceptive sleep so we will have knowledge of self, and knowledge of life purpose.

It is fascinating that friendship is formed and found under the strangest circumstances. We may look like the odd couple, but we are meant to be there to help each other through tough times. Until we understand our roles as keepers of one another, we will fail as sisters because of a common bond we are bound to each other by our souls. I believe that there is a spiritual intensification, a mental and emotional awakening that is shaking many sisters loose from their ignorance, self-deception, and group divisions. There's an urgent need to break free of the chains that have kept us passive, apathetic, and afraid. We're so tired of feeling sick, weary, lonely, depressed, and unfulfilled. So we ask ourselves, "Is this all there is to life?"

Sister-to-Sister: Why me? Because I am strong. Why me? Because I am in a position to help others. Why me? Because I overcame certain situations. Why me? Because the grace of God covers me and allow me to rise above the bad things. Why me? Because I am here for a reason, and every day I still learn good reasons to answer my question: Why me?

The Woman In The Mirror vs. The Woman Within

*"In being authentic, we not only honor ourselves
—we offer a gift to whomever we deal with."*

Foundation is a cosmetic base for makeup, but later in the chapter we will talk about a life changing foundation to build upon. Basically, we use makeup for these three reasons:

1. **To cover up what we don't want seen**

2. **To make up for what we think we don't have**

3. **To enhance what we want noticed**

In our society, we spend a lot of time wearing masks. We think that we can control the woman in the mirror easier than the one within. We love to dress ourselves up, stand in front of the mirror, and ask others how we look? What do you think? And based on their opinion, you make your decision to wear a particular style or a certain color. And as long as it or they flatter us, we are happy. We wonder why girls as young as five years old have an issue about how they look. It's because they watch and imitate you. Whoever came up with the idea of Barbie was struggling with identification issues. How else would you make a toy that looks better than you, dresses better, and has more accessories than you have. Barbie has her own car and beach house and a perfect man named Ken. We are just a group of women trying to be like a doll that should have been made to look like you and me in the first place. If you were to give her a few extra pounds, hair that's not manageable, clothes she can't afford, a minivan instead of a convertible and an imperfect man like Adam, then you would be able to relate. As long as you keep making her up in your mind, you will always deal with low self-worth because you can't and never will live up to that image. So we spend too much time trying to be something we were never meant to be. Yes, this chapter is bitter sweet. But it has to be to provoke you into recognizing the woman within and give her some credit for being a beautiful woman with attributes such has being creative, passionate, forgiving, humble, courageous, sympathetic, intelligent, strong and the list goes on and on. I'm not naive to the fact that some of you have been molested, raped, beaten, verbally abused, abandoned and hurt beyond words.

Sister-to-Sister: At four years old, the fifteen-year-old son of a friend of the family molested me. For many years I could not understand why I felt so uncomfortable when I saw an older child with a younger female child. This mystery was solved when the memory bubble burst and I felt like I was going to throw up my inside. The sickness of pushed away pain can be unbearable when awakened.

Will Thy Be Made Whole? Yes Lord, Make Me Whole.

"Character is the outside appurtenance of what's on the inside."

We as women are critical, judgmental and intimidated by one another. How do you see other women. Are they approachable for conversation, friendship? Has a sister ever hurt you or betrayed you? If so, how did you deal with it? These are important questions to ask yourself because we can't allow anything or anyone to compromise who we are as a person. What is inside of women that causes us to be sad, lonely, bitter, angry, hateful or spiteful? Don't get upset, because you know what I'm saying is true. We all want to quote the scripture about the virtuous woman, but I'm digging for the real woman. I say to you, come out, come out wherever you are. I'm calling you out sister because I know what's locked up inside of you has made you tired of being ashamed, prideful, lonely, and hurting and wanting to give up. If that's you, I want you to know by the anointing of God. I have been called to speak life to you, so you will let go of that that rotten stuff that has attached itself to your soul and does not allow you to come out of where you are. It is essential that you do, because I'm not complete without you.

The Thirsty Woman

"Regardless of race and age, women can sense who they can talk to."

The story of the woman at the well tells us that she came every day to the well to gather water after the other women had finished and went on their way. No doubt she was dealing with low self-worth. But I wonder what the outcome would have been if one sister had waited there for her. Not to condemn her or judge her or try to get close to her to find out her business. If you had met her, what would you have said? I can imagine my conversation would have gone something like this: "Hello my sister. My name is Kim and I've waited here to have a heart to heart girl talk with you. Let me start by sharing what's been in my secret closet that's covered up with shame and regret, things that are so painfully private that the mere thought of dredging them up scares me. I now know that most of the situations I found myself in were because I didn't know who I was." I can imagine tears beginning to run down her face and she looks at me with sympathy and compassion because she now sees hope in the horizon. She can relate to seeing herself in me. Her trust has been won. Now she will allow me to help her. From your positioning of where you are right now as a whole woman, I would like for you to write down what you would say to her. You meet her every day, but you haven't learned how to recognize her. Just remember, she looks like you.

Sister-to-Sister: I never thought that at forty-seven I would still be a virgin. Like most single women, I wonder if I will ever find the right man. I am not necessarily looking for a shining knight, but a man who's an achiever with compassion, sensitivity, and discipline, and has a need for a deeper meaning in life. Not a perfect man, just a man perfect for me.

He Saw the Best In You.

"There's only one corner of the universe you can be certain of improving, and that's your own self"—Aldous Huxley

I know you were told you wouldn't make it or you will never amount to anything, that you are not worthy of love, you are not educated, not pretty enough, too fat or too thin, you talk funny and on and on. And to add insult to injury, you may have been told those things by people you love – your family and friends. But God saw the best in you, even when everyone else around could only see the worst in you. Without the Lord, you would have lost your mind and ended it all. But God had an escape plan for you. Have you ever thought that maybe the storm is not for the Lord to bring you out, but for him to come in? We have to learn to utilize information, life lessons, and healing techniques that will help us to fill a void in ourselves. The problem that so many women deal with is low self-esteem. It may seem small and insignificant by name, but it can hinder every area of your life.

It is cancer to our souls and makes us believe that God can't love us or use us for His glory. The majority of people with low self-esteem are women. You need to realize how smart, beautiful, and wonderfully made you are. Think of all of the things you are capable of – making and giving life, nourishing a child, being someone's rock and shelter. Someone in this world needs you and loves you just the way you are. Why not add another person to that list – you. What is self-esteem? You are the only person on the planet who can establish, build and nurture your self-esteem. You are the only one who is in charge of creating a prosperous happy life and to take control over your actions, decisions and emotions in your life. Self-esteem is your control, your approach toward the "attacks" of reality. Your self-esteem is your appraisal, your evaluation and your feelings about yourself. It is your opinion of the person who you have been living with since you were born, yourself. A negative self-image creates massive stressors in your life because you are always in doubt, never feeling like you fit in and never thinking you are good enough. Your esteem is one of the hardest things to build and one of the easiest to lose. It can be damaged by the negativity thrown your way by people you allow in your life. Raising your self-esteem is about transforming your life from depression, fear and uncertainty to happiness, confidence and joy!

Feeling good about yourself expands to form a solid foundation for your actions, your thought patterns, your speech, your posture, your attitude with which you face the challenges of the world around you, as well as your ability to make positive decisions that will be beneficial for you in the future. Self-confidence and self-esteem are related. The more confidence you have, the higher the level of your self-esteem. Self-confidence techniques help you to better take care of yourself, to create a strong base (**foundation**) for your self-esteem and to live in peace with your inner self.

Steps to Developing Self-esteem

1. **Start with the small things.** Take small steps and make small choices to gain confidence in your ability to make a decision. As you become secure in your ability to make good choices, you will gain confidence in yourself, and be more secure about your abilities in general.

2. **Don't always try to please others.** It is considerate to care about others' feelings, but your needs are important, too. Do not try to be like someone else, either. You will be at your best when you are being yourself because of your uniqueness. Strive to be your best, and do not criticize yourself if you fall short of your expectations.

3. **Avoid negative people.** People who have a negative attitude that may rub off on you are not good for you. If you're timid, loud and aggressive, people are probably not good for you, and vice versa. Whatever you do, do not compare yourself to others. Just be the best that you can be.

4. **Face your fears and learn from your failures.** We only fail when we do not make the best out of adversity. When something doesn't go the way we would like it to, there is something to be learned from that, which can be applied next time you are in a similar situation. Get up and try again.

5. **Don't worry about being "perfect."** Aiming for perfection in life is a lost cause because it is different things to different people. Nobody is perfect in the eyes of everyone else, so by trying to be perfect, you may just be setting yourself up for disappointment and failure. Instead, seek to achieve small goals that you have set.

Self-Esteem Test

"If you want the rainbow, you've got to put up with the rain."

This self-esteem test is quick and simple. Answer TRUE or FALSE to each question. (If you cannot answer 100% TRUE, then answer FALSE - check below how to score.):

1. Other people are not better off or more fortunate than I am.

2. I accept myself as I am and am happy with myself.

3. I enjoy socializing.

4. I deserve love and respect.

5. I feel valued and needed.

6. I don't need others to tell me I have done a good job.

7. Being myself is important.

8. I make friends easily.

9. I can accept criticism without feeling put down.

10. I admit my mistakes openly.

11. I never hide my true feelings.

12. I always speak up for myself and put my views across.

13. I am a happy, carefree person.

14. I don't worry what others think of my views.

15. I don't need others' approval to feel good.

16. I don't feel guilty about _____ .

TEST SCORE: Total number of TRUE answers you gave, EACH ONE POINT:
    15-16 Points - You have a high level of self-esteem!
    12-14 Points - Not bad, but there's room for you to improve.
    8-11 Points - Low self-esteem is holding you back.
    Below 8 Points - Your esteem is drastically low!

Sister-to-Sister: Some of us never associate the love of self with the same importance we stress on the love of another. It's truly a simple concept. How can you love someone else if you don't love yourself? Ask yourself who is the most important person to you. If the answer isn't you, then we have a problem.

Be assertive. Boosting your self-esteem is all about getting what you need/want. So do things for your own sake. Remember, you must help yourself first before you can help others. You can't lose or give away what you don't have, so be selfish and when you come to a higher level within yourself, you can start helping others with lower self-esteem. And at the end, only you will recollect what you have done, define who you are and what you're about.

Don't Count Me Out.

"The time will come when all you can do is pick yourself up and continue your journey."

Who I am is not the woman I desire to be. I know you have me out and down for the count, but you can't keep a woman down. **Count 1** – I'm facing down on the floor. It's agonizing because I'm dealing with some crucial issues. **Wait !** – I'm on my knees, not two but one, holed up. I'm in a kneeling position. God has heard my cry and saw my pain. **Count 3** – I'm up on my feet. Praise God! I may be bruised, but thank God I'm not broken.

I would like to recognize all women who are on their journey to healing. Know that you are not alone. We are right here with you.

I pray every woman will awaken to a brighter day when she can finally hear her own heart beat, strong and vibrant, echoing, "I know I'm a whole woman of God."

ABOUT THE AUTHOR

Debora D. Taylor

Debora D. Taylor the founder and President of the Taylor Made International Institute in Milwaukee, Wisconsin has been an inspiring and integral leader in the human service field for over 25 years with expertise in the areas of women issues, marriage and family enrichment, youth, early childhood and responsible fatherhood. An inspirational role model, mentor, trainer and teacher, who take a proactive engaging, approach to all she does. Debora is a proficient and skilled educator, and facilitator, certified trainer and consultant in both the secular and faith based communities. She has effectively integrated her passion for serving with her interdisciplinary education to develop several popular and interactive trainings, workshops, seminars and retreats for culturally diverse populations, through out the United States.

Ms.Taylor has a special interest in and talent for addressing the needs of families ,including issues such as serving individuals experiencing economic disadvantage, involving fathers and extended family members and helping people identify their self worth and talents. By working with families directly and serving on various committees and boards at the local, state and regional levels Debora has contributed her wisdom and expertise on the issues most relevant to the women, fathers and families for whom she so deeply cares. For her efforts, her enthusiasm and her great successes she continues to be recognize locally and nationally.

Ms. Taylor received her formal education from Milwaukee Theological Institute and Springfield College graduating with honors *cum laude* with a Bachelor of Science degree in Human Services. She is member of the Professional Woman Network Speakers Bureau and a certified trainer.

Among her many accomplishments she is an ordained minister and co –pastors New Life Kingdom Ministries Church with her husband Guy. They have two successful young adult children Nyshi Shateya and Dominique Lamar Wayne. The love of her life is My'Asha *(which means God's Blessing)* Nyshateya her granddaughter.

Published Articles
Co Author of Bruised but Not Broken Released Date August 13, 2010
Professional Spotlight
2009 Co-Host of the "Fathers Strengthening Families" Radio Show AM 1290 Milwaukee

Certifications /Special Trainings
Professional Women Network Trainer: Woman's Issues, Leadership Skills for Women, The Assertive Woman, Woman in Management, Life Skills for Women, and the Superwoman Syndrome.

Helen Bader Non –Profit Management and Leadership Certificate, Young Father Parenting Curriculum, Family Service Credential Master Trainer's Level, Exploring Parenting, Grandparent Support Trainer, 24-7 Dads, PREP © Christian PREP © "PREP © "Within My Reach" Christian PREP© African –American Marriage Enrichment Curriculum © Black Marriage Curriculum for Couples© Prepare-Enrich, Family Wellness, How to Avoid Marrying a Jerk/Jerkette Curriculums LoveU2 / Love Notes (Youth)

Activities and Awards:
Wisconsin Head Start Association Board Member
Region V Head Start Board Member
Milwaukee Fatherhood Collaborative Board Member
Mayor's Milwaukee Fatherhood Initiative Registration Committee Chairperson
Milwaukee Marriage Partnership Network/ *(Faith Partnership Network)*
King Advisory Inc. Board of Directors
National Black Child Development Association Board of Directors (Milwaukee Affiliate)
Proclamations from the Milwaukee County Supervisor and City of Milwaukee Mayor's Offices for Outstanding Community Service
Featured Marriage Educator in the Annie E. Casey Foundation Publication: Healthy Marriages in Low Income African –American Communities *(Purple Edition)*

NINE

THE ART OF BEING REAL: TAKE OFF THE MASK

By Pastor Debora Taylor

My precious Sistas – as the chapters unfold within the pages of *Bruised But Not Broken,* all of us will begin an inner healing process, no matter how deep the pain, by admitting it and acknowledging that some of the most unimaginable stories made us vulnerable to being real. The Art of Being Real: Take off the Mask will mean many things to different women. Open your heart to the journey.

The Invitation

My Dearest Sista – I would like to extend an invitation for you to be my guest at the "King of Kings, Keeping it Real" masquerade ball. I was assigned by the King to plan this wonderful occasion. Throwing beautiful events and gatherings is something I love to do. I guarantee, my sistas, you will not be disappointed. You must promise while being my guest that you will be very observant and take notes along the way.

These normal, average, clever, dynamic, intelligent sistas have done some pretty crazy things while being protected by the anonymity of a mask. Now, as we enter the masquerade ball... Oh, I forgot to tell you we are debutantes, part of the King's Court, so pay close attention to our sistas's behavior and really listen to the story behind the masks. Our King is relying on us to scan the crowd for an accurate report. Here are some questions we must answer. How many are hurting at a deep level? How many are too stressed to realize they are really blessed and they are the apple of the King's eye. How many are struggling with physical, emotional, toxic and unhealthy personal and professional relationships with men, women and their immediate family.

Ok, Here's the Royal Court. Let's Get Ready With Pen and Paper and Get to Work.

Sista Unloved is wearing a great looking, yet simple but, chic mask. She wears a beautiful scarlet red ballroom gown. It represents the scars of her childhood. Our encounter with her is deep emotional pain. She personally knows the Kings of Kings, yet she feels too dirty and unworthy to let Him come in completely and live within her. She knows the saying, "Greater is He that is Within Me."

Next, down the aisle comes Sista 3 P, known as the **Sista of Position, Power and Pride**. She is bigheaded, high-minded, haughty, and exclusive in her interactions with others. She is really covering up her own feelings of insecurity with a hard exterior. Wearing a stunning royal purple ball gown and platinum mask trimmed in diamonds, she accomplishes her goal to stand out in the crowd. She is the belle of the ball and seems to have it all together. But does she really?

Entering the masquerade ball is **Sista Activity…….. Always Busy**. Our Sista is dressed like an angel in a snow-white ball gown, with a first-class matching feathered mask trimmed in lace covering her entire face. She could be the overachiever in her personal and professional life. Everything she touches turns into gold. Maybe she's the wife and mother with a picture perfect house, husband and kids. Or perhaps, a single mother doing everything by herself with no assistance from anyone and doing a fine job. When you ask her how she is doing, she immediately says, fine. Yet, she keeps moving because if she stops, we will find out she is a mask-hider, full of commotion, yet never still. Loads of potential locked inside, but too busy to allow God to reach inside that deep place that only the Spirit of the Lord knows. Although she hears the words "Be Still and Know I am God," she cannot stop because then we will know her emptiness.

Our Sistas, dressed up their scars, pain and criticisms to attend the masquerade ball, are listening and eyeballing the crowd for an imparting word to be spoken into their lives. Lord, we know your unconditional love transforms our resistance, to disclose and expose those things that have kept my sistas unable to be their real selves. The childhood scars, hard exterior and the emptiness are cover-ups to what is really going on in the lives of these sistas. Let them draw nigh to you, oh Lord, through their personal prayers and mediation. Our conclusions? Send your angels of healing and love to set them free from all the bondages of the facades that have been maintained.

The Beginning of Our Masquerade

As African American sistas, many of us battle with trust, confidence, closeness and encouragement in our relationship journey. Our ethnic circle teaches us to use emotional anesthesia to conceal our pain. We have the tenacity to choose wisely with whom we will reveal our inner selves to because of the battle of these unbiblical proverbs, "What is said in this house, stays in this house. What is said in this family, stays in this family." These voices set in motion what I call the "Keeping Family Business Restriction Cycle," which begins the intergenerational masquerade ball. We African American sistas must often remind ourselves that we must keep the mask of our family business, which serves to lead us into denial or destructive patterns that have plagued our families for generations.

Although the Word of God says in Psalms 139: 14, *"I will praise you for I am fearfully and wonderfully made,"* as women, we can be totally vulnerable and dependent on the comments and opinions around us. We absorb everything folks tell us, both positive and negative. We internalize other individual's reactions to our actions and measure ourselves accordingly. Hiding behind a mask makes the risk of disclosure less terrifying.

Growing up Sis, we embrace these beliefs, but keep them hidden because we don't want anyone else to know! We create an image of ourselves that is different from and usually better than the person we believe we are. Most of us do it one time or another – we "try on" different masks to see which is the most comfortable, which affords us the most protection from exposure. We put on a mask that shows the world a different face and hide behind it for as long as possible. That's what these three sistas attending the masquerade ball have done, but

I believe they all want one main thing. It is to come from behind the mask and be real.

Most people would say, "I am a pretty straight forward, really down to earth sista. The realness in my life began and my personal walk in faith helped me to understand His original intent for my existence was to be a blessing by becoming a spiritual midwife to sistas. My healing occurs as I realize and verbalize to myself, to mature mentors and the Lord, the beliefs and actions that maintain my painful existence and keep me bound. Many unpleasant destructive voices had plagued my life. Yet, the voices taught me how to hold on, be strong and push forward. My destructive rage and anger was changed to a hunger and thirst for righteousness and realness. My fears turned into tears of compassion to assist my sistas to move toward inner healing that will bring completeness in their lives."

The Art of Being Real is "**R**eaching an **E**arnest and **A**uthentic **L**ife." No matter what obstacles you face, reach out for the King of Kings, for the will of God in your life. Are you willing to empty yourself of hidden agendas, private yearnings, and secret hopes and dreams, so that the King might pour His unconditional love into your life?

Listening to the Voices of Our Sistas

Many sistas have a deep desire to seek inner healing, yet too often the greatest hindrance to being real is not others, but it is us being real with ourselves. My healing continues as I share the realness of my life situations. It helps to bring emotional wholeness. Encouraging sistas to keep eliminating the various masks in their lives and assisting them professionally and personally in understanding the depth of their masquerade can determine your own destiny. Our process of realness can be hard and long, especially when we harbor our hurts like cherished possessions. Take the seat of honor, allow the King to transform and undress the layers of years and tears of the outward show. He is speaking through the many voices of our sistas...............

Listen to the voice of our Sista.......

I wore a mask for many years doing whatever anyone ask me to do, trying to fit in with everyone to make other people happy...not caring about myself...always caring for others. In order for me to stop wearing a mask, I had to be real with myself ,and start caring about me. That's when the mask started coming off....the more real you become, the more masks will come off..... Being Real is knowing who you are, being your real self, and doing things that make you happy.....Enjoying life and knowing what makes you happy.... All in All, keeping it real... You being you is Real Enough ..... Pam

My definition for the mask is, "**M**asquerading the **A**gonies of our **S**uffering with the **K**iss of Life," like a frame holding a painting that has the various textures and brush strokes of our lives. We step out with our beautiful smiles, stylish clothes, learning to wear the outer garment of our pain to paint a canvass that all is right with the world. But many times, this is not our story.

Listen to the voice of our Sista............

Artists paint on many canvasses, using multiple tools and color palettes. Life from the time of conception has different stages and phrases, some healthy, some unhealthy, but it all formulates into our being or becoming..... The Art of Being Real ...... is taking the mask off and is a portrait of transparency in the midst of pain, suffering, adversity, esteem issues, abuse and life transitions. Being able to take off or put off that which comes to discolor one's views of one's true self of love, expressions and receiving without pretending to be other than who you were created to be...... Sherrie

God uses a diversity of the artist's instruments to draw out the authentic areas in our lives. Each woman is different and unique. You are an original, my beloved Sista. No one is like you. Some of us have to allow the King to dig a little deeper as our lives jump off the canvass and to become a piece of clay in the Potter's hands. Molding and shaping us into a beautiful sculpture, in spite of our imperfections.

Listen to our Sista.......

Removing the false identity of being Ghetto fabulous, somebody's baby mama, fighting with myself instead of being the woman I was born to be ..... being lost in a cloud of darkness, instead of being the Black Beautiful Woman God created me to be. When you finally let go and let God remove and recreate the new vase God intended you to be, you become that wife, lover, sister, co-worker, a healer, a provider. A Woman that can tell you how to be a Real Woman and not a person somebody wants you to be ...... A'Raea

As we listen to the voices of our sistas, a similar theme rings true. Our real power comes when we simply be ourselves and walk with the King of Kings. Remember, removing some masks is a tremendous task requiring forethought and determination because of the many different faces we as women have had to wear. In closing, if you are in a relationship with a sista who seeks to discontinue the masquerade, offer her an empathic ear, compassion and love.

Sista Reflections

Remembrance: Recall the cost in your personal and professional life of wearing a mask. How are/were your relationships affected? How do/did you keep up your image? What limitations were created? What would be the significance of taking off the mask?

Recognition: In your own words, describe "The Art of Being Real: Take off the Mask." Think about your mask – how it looks to you and other people when you put it on and take it off. What do you steal from yourself when you live a life of wearing a disguise? What are you willing to surrender in order to walk in realness and wholeness?

Realization: Realize the mask is not who you are. The mask has served its purpose and now it is only an obstacle to your maturity and contentment.

Responsibility: Be willing to take the responsibility to change each of your masks, personally and professionally.

Radical: Decide to do whatever it takes to become the real, genuine, authentic, and bona fide you.

Notes:

_____

_____

_____

_____

_____

_____

_____

_____

_____

_____

_____

_____

_____

_____

_____

_____

_____

_____

_____

_____

ABOUT THE AUTHOR

MONICA MAY

Monica May is the host of the Tom Joyner Morning Show, as well as News/Community Affairs Director at STAR 94.5 a COX Radio station in Orlando, FL. She's been in the radio and television business for 30 years and this is actually her second time in the Sunshine State. Monica moved back from Houston, TX where she was the media relations director for a faith based non-profit organization that worked specifically with the homeless population. In fact, besides her current job as news anchor at STAR "Working with the homeless and managing a $4 million housing project for that population, have been the highlights of my career!" says Ms. May. Because of her concern and generosity to community projects such as that, Monica is often called the *"HARDEST WORKING WOMAN IN RADIO."*

Monica obtained her B.S. Degree in Speech Communication from the State University of New York at Brockport and has worked in radio and television since 1979 in a variety of cities, such as Atlanta, New Orleans and Washington D.C. She has also worked as a correspondent with Black Entertainment Television (B.E.T.).

Ms. May has received the Outstanding Reporter Award from the Florida Public Health Association; Top 25 Women in Orlando-Women's History Project; Parent of the Year-N.A.A.C.P.; Urban Radio Programming, and many others. She is a member of the Central Florida Black Journalists and The Houston Black Public Relations Society. Ms. May is a professional speaker and has also founded her own businesses; **Consider Your Image and SPEAK EASY 1**, which provide media coaching and workshop facilitation.

Just named an Orlando Magic Maker for her contributions to the Central Florida community, Monica's professional objective is to "remain in the forefront of women making a difference in communication through public interaction, involvement and community leadership".

Contact:
monicamayandassociates@gmail.com

TEN

FEELING THE LIFE WITHIN

By Monica May

I t's hard to believe now how long I went before I even realized that I had anything inside me, let alone *life within*. I would have to say that from the time I can remember until about 31, I just lived life, if you know what I mean. There was no zest, no direction. Sure there were times when I was motivated, like during college and shortly after I graduated and got my first job. But after losing that job in less than a year, I was back to just "ho-humming" it through life. I look back now and can't even believe I've made it this far. I realize now that there really was a purpose for my life and that it would take trial, error, and tragedy before I could really say, "Yes, I Can Feel the Life Within."

If you're a mother, I'm sure you can remember the first time you felt the flutter of your baby in that first trimester. Once they were born, how about the first time you heard them cry? Imagine how it was for them to hear their own voice? Notice how as soon as a baby hears its own voice they begin to shriek, or even cry just to hear themselves? They learn to amuse themselves and manipulate us all at the same time.

My own daughter was destined to be a talker. At least that's what the doctor said when I took her in for excessive crying. Yes, I took my baby girl to the doctor because she seemed to cry *all* the time. You see, I had prayed all throughout my pregnancy that my own sadness and constant crying over the breakup with her father wouldn't affect her. So now you understand why I took her in. I thought that I had damaged her in some way because it seemed like nothing seemed to satisfy my newborn and I didn't want to do anything that was harmful. They just said she's simply expressing herself. So from that time on I just allowed her to express herself by crying, shrieking or whatever.

Imagine your own life with that freedom. The freedom that whenever you spoke, someone listened and responded. Adults don't have that ability – or so we think. In the boardroom or the bedroom, we feel suppressed, like no one's listening. Or what we have to say is falling on deaf ears. But, just how are you using your voice? Do you whine when you think you can get away with it? I'll bet you stand there and shriek when things aren't going your way. Or do you yell, with fire and venom in your voice when you really want to make your point? Guess what, those decibels of demand won't mean a thing if the other person doesn't feel your sincerity. It's just as a child can sense the goodness in a person, so can another human being when they think you're really passionate. So, just how are you getting your point across?

For years I thought I was invisible. I mean, as a child, no one paid any attention to me or what I had to say. I remember the first time an adult *really* looked at me and listened to what I had to say. I was about six years old. I can't remember who it was, only that I was amazed that an adult had actually paid attention to me. From that time on, although I remained a basically shy person, I've used my voice as a means of not only communicating, but connecting with people.

Today, I'm a radio announcer and I connect with hundreds of thousands of people daily. But if you had asked me as a young person if I would be on the radio one day, I would have looked upon you strangely. I didn't think I had anything to say that people would ever listen to or a presence that would make people respond. I had no idea of who I was or that I really did possess a spark, a voice or a *life within* that was waiting to be released. Believe it or not, we all do! In fact, take a moment to think about what you sound like when you're trying to make a point.

How do you think you sound to your kids if you don't think they're "getting you?" Is it a shriek followed by demands?

_____

_____

What about to your husband or boyfriend?

_____

_____

How about at work?

_____

_____

Your decibel of demand anchored with how confident you sound (with those demands) will determine how serious anyone will take you. Don't believe me? Try using a soft, insecure voice when asking someone to do something for you and see how quickly they respond. There's a certain vibrato that has to come with your intention. What does your voice and sincerity have to do with *feeling the life within?* Before you can feel the life within you, you have to know what you're looking for.

Part of the *life within* has to do with realizing your self-esteem. How much do you believe that you should have whatever it is you're asking of someone else? If you truly believe in yourself and what you're asking, then you probably believe whole heartedly that you should receive it, right? Well let's take an unscientific look at self-esteem. I always say that if a person is born healthy, they have five natural senses (sight, smell, taste, hearing and touch). However, the one sense that can take you through life is self-esteem. It is a developed sense, one that is encouraged in you as a young child and enhanced as you grow older. However, many of you may have never had the encouragement to develop a healthy self-esteem. Without that sense of self, the confidence to be who you are takes a lot longer to shine.

Many of you reading this book may have suffered abuse at an early age. You've been bruised along the way, but let me tell you – you're definitely NOT BROKEN. For instance, if you had a parent who was an alcoholic, you may have lived in a household where you were always on edge. If your parent was physically or verbally abusive, you may have grown up trying to make yourself as invisible as possible, just to stay out of the "line of fire." Or if you were like me, my mom wasn't an alcoholic, nor did she abuse me physically or verbally, but if you remember, I said for a long time I thought I was invisible. I now believe that comes from simply being ignored. I don't believe it was intentional, but it was just that way in our household.

I came along when my parent's marriage wasn't going so well. There was often a lot of yelling that I remember, even as a child. I was young, but I also remember a lot of sadness in our house after my father left. From that moment on, my mother went into survival mode and that didn't include cuddling or even laughing with my sister and me. She had to keep a roof over our heads and that meant we were on our own.

Now, I'm not saying we were neglected. We had our basic needs met, there was always food and we were clean. But I never really remember any hugs or being told, "I love you." The fact that my dad was gone not only gave me a really empty feeling, but it was also an equation for disaster. You can bet I spent most of my life seeking that human touch and searching everywhere just to hear those three simple words. Does that sound familiar to you? I'll bet there are many women who were brought up in that same situation and went in search of something that would fill that void.

I know for me it was a void that I filled with alcohol, drugs and men. It took a long time to admit that I was searching for something. I thought I was just having fun. I realize now that my low self-esteem (or really no esteem) was the root of it all. Let's take a moment to look at self-esteem.

To paraphrase Nathaniel Branden, PhD in an article from "The Art of Living Consciously," he tells us *What Self-Esteem Is and Is Not...* He defines self-esteem as being competent enough to cope with the basic challenges of life and of being worthy of happiness. He also says, "Self-esteem is not temporarily induced by a drug, a compliment, or a love affair." Dr. Branden claims that if it's not grounded in reality, or built over time through the appropriate operation of mind, then it's not self-esteem.

With that being said, what do you define self-esteem as?

_____

_____

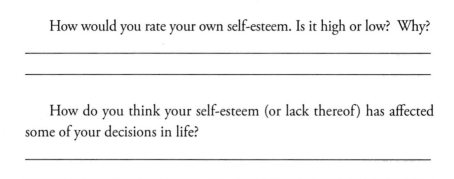

How would you rate your own self-esteem. Is it high or low? Why?

_____

_____

How do you think your self-esteem (or lack thereof) has affected some of your decisions in life?

_____

_____

I'd like to think that we all would make better decisions knowing now what we think we know about self-esteem. But remember, the good doctor's definition said, "Self-esteem is not temporarily induced by a drug, a compliment, or a love affair." Hmm, aren't those all the things I was searching for? You bet and I wasn't alone. That journey took me down many back alleys and I saw a lot of horrible things that still haunt me. I've seen people killed, beaten badly and I've even visited a dear friend who couldn't take what this life had to offer and decided to take his own. Watching someone linger for days after shooting themselves in the head is awful. I can't help thinking how that could have been me at any time. But even after all of that, I still searched.

I stayed in those streets for years. Sure, I was able to maintain a job, an apartment, and even look like I had it all together; it was sad. What was so sad is that I couldn't figure out for the life of me what I was searching for. There wasn't enough alcohol, the high didn't last long enough and there wasn't a man with endurance to stand up to me or ask me what was I looking for? I'm not even sure I could have even put it into words. How about you?

Have you ever been in that situation? Explain.

_____

_____

Has there ever been a time in your life where you were doing things that you knew that you shouldn't have been doing? What were they?

_____

_____

If so, why do you think you were doing them? i.e. What do you think you were searching for?

_____

_____

For me, I believe a lot of my search was based in closure. I realize now that I also have attachment issues. Think about it, my father left when I was a little girl and I only saw him on rare occasions. He left at a time when all I could think of was what I might have done to make him leave. Isn't that something? Think about it. Isn't that what most little girls think when their daddies leave them? Isn't that why most of us are out there searching? We're looking for the love of our fathers. You've heard this before. As sisters, we are on our hands and knees at times crying out for our dads at the hands of abusive situations with men and other lovers.

My *light* moment came for me twenty years ago after I gave birth to the most beautiful baby girl in the world. I had a rocky relationship with her father and unfortunately, after trying hard to make it work for the sake of our baby, I had to realize that after all of the crying and pleading, it just wasn't going to work. Somehow I thought I just might be the one to break that cycle, but it wasn't to be. Anyway, I had a great pregnancy, but as soon as I delivered, something went terribly wrong and I was taken back in for surgery. To this day, I believe it was God's way of getting my attention. I stayed in the hospital for ten days and went home only to hemorrhage and come back to the emergency room. A second surgery determined the bleeding was because the full placenta had been left in me. I could have died. I don't believe in mistakes, only miracles and when I came out of surgery, I was clear on my reason to live. I asked my mother to bring my Bible and I opened it to Romans 8:18. *"Consider that the sufferings of this present time are not worthy to be compared with the glory which shall be revealed in us."*

My light within shines brightly today. And yes, I've been bruised, but never broken. Even when my soul cries out for a man, I realize the goodness that comes from my Father. I have a peace today that surpasses all understanding. I don't ever want to forget the rough times I've endured. In fact, those thoughts help to keep me in touch with other teen sisters and women I speak to across the country. And Lord knows my past helps me stay in tune with the hundreds of thousands of listeners I talk to daily on the radio. My job is awesome. I'm still baffled, even after 30 years, that I can get behind a microphone and do amazing things and make connections with others just like you.

Notes:

_____

_____

_____

_____

_____

_____

_____

_____

_____

_____

_____

_____

_____

_____

_____

_____

_____

_____

_____

_____

_____

_____

ABOUT THE AUTHOR

CHARLOTTE RANDOLPH

 Charlotte Randolph is an Entrepreneur by design. She is an owner of several businesses. Being the CEO of Dynamic Empowerment LLC, her mission is to empower women, youth, and families. She also works for one of the largest health care systems in the State of Wisconsin as a Parent Educator. Her educational background is in Early Childhood Education. She is also a certified trained facilitator for Stewards of Children, a child sexual abuse prevention training. Ms.Randolph conducts parenting classes with a specialty in nurturing programs as a certified facilitator. She is a woman of compassion and believes in protecting and promoting the well-being of children. As a Certified Diversity Consultant with special emphasis in women's issues, she conducts several seminars to empower women and make individuals aware of diversity. Teaching with no limits is her model. Ms.Randolph will educate everyone who treads across her path. She will genuinely make you feel like you important because you are. She is a peacemaker and a great friend to many. If you are ready for an encounter with a phenomenal woman, then you need to contact Dynamic Empowerment, LLC.

As the President and CEO of Apple Tree Educational Services LLC, she conducts continuing educational class for caregivers, providers, and early childhood teachers. She is the Executive Director of and early childhood center that serves children from birth to thirteen years of age. Being a certified Teen Image Coach she is able to make a positive impact on the youth who attends her workshops, seminars and retreats. Charlotte Randolph knows first hand how to overcome and conquer your dreams and turn them into your reality. She is greatly honored to have received two of her certifications from The Professional Women Network and is a co-author of many books being released in 2010 through the Professional Woman Publishing.

Contact:
Dynamic Empowerment LLC,
P.O. Box 080611
Milwaukee, Wisconsin 53208
(414) 915-9546
dynamicempowerment@att.net

ELEVEN

AIN'T NO WHERE TO GO BUT UP

By Charlotte Randolph

From early childhood I witnessed physical abuse which tormented my young child's mind. The impression the experience made can bring me to tears this very day. I was at the bottom and hoping for the top. My adolescent years brought even more pain by being manipulated and preyed upon by men. I couldn't find a way to stand up and say **"No! Stop! Get Away!"** As a woman, I can look back on my past and embrace the pain but realize that it was up to me to start the journey from the bottom to the top.

I took back the power that was stolen from me when I realized that Earth has no sorrows that heaven cannot heal. Being bruised by words, thoughts, and rejection can break your spirit, but it can heal. A broken spirit is like having a broken wing. You can't fly with a spirit of brokenness. You cannot soar with a heavy heart. Eagles fly high. When you fly, **ain't nowhere to go but up!** Your vision has to be clear enough to see what you need to survive. I called this an eagle's eye. I needed to have this clear 'eagle's vision' about my life and realize that I was more than just my circumstances! I had allowed people to bring me down. I thought that what they said about me was more valuable than my own opinion. I allowed their thoughts to rule me.

Sticks and Stones may Break my Bones

I wanted to be accepted by my peers and family. I wanted everybody to love me. Between the ages of 7-12 I stopped loving myself. I know you have heard the saying, **"Sticks and stones may break my bones but words will never hurt me."** This statement is partially the truth. Words do hurt and I allowed them to break my heart and my spirit. At the tender age of seven I was called all types of names and it hurt my very being. It made me question my presence. When I looked at myself, I was perfect. My body image was just right. The hurt and rejection came when people made jokes about me. It changed my whole view of myself. I was called "Pocha" that stood for "Poor child." I was told I had a big forehead, buck teeth and was skinny. I thought I was perfect. People would laugh when those who were close to me talked about me in that manner. This would hurt me to my core because I thought they loved me. I started to look at myself very closely and bought into what they were saying about me. I believed all these things and accepted it as my imperfections. Life at that time was very confusing. I would hear someone saying positive things about me and that built me back up. Then I would turn around and someone would tear me back down with something negative. I wish I could have blocked out all the negative words because there is power in words, deeds, and actions! Your thoughts are just as powerful.

The things that healed my broken pieces were the things I enjoyed the most. I danced, sung, and played hard. I became a leader. I created things that brought joy to others and me. I would talk to the elders and gain so much knowledge. I also learned how not to react to the negative comments and stay out of the midst of ignorance.

When the Predators Come

As a woman today, I understand that I was manipulated as a teenager. I did not understand the opposite sex nor did I know what love was. I grew up in a household with an abusive stepfather until the age of about eleven years old. My biological father died when I was twelve and the predators of destruction came very quickly. At the age of fourteen I dated my first actual boyfriend who was five years older and that relationship lasted until I was seventeen. I lost so much of my youth during those years and experienced enough drama for a lifetime. If only I had known how to protect myself against the whispers. My life was altered during this period. I believe this individual was no good for not only me, but also himself. He lied about who he was and how old he was. He portrayed to be someone who cared about me and wanted to be with me, but I knew during that period that the relationship was not what God wanted for me. I thank God for another chance. I was innocent and preyed upon. I thought I knew everything, but actually knew absolutely nothing to prevent this situation from happening.

Moving On

The Lord's word states that He will never leave you nor forsake you. As that chapter closed in my life and I was out of that relationship, I began to realize that I learned a lot. My whole life experience from childhood to adolescence equipped me for what I would become today. What the Devil meant for evil, God turned around for my good. Oh yes, I was bruised, but definitely not broken. The wind may have blown and knocked me down, but while I was down I was going to pray. Victory was mine, regardless of the circumstances. Do I wish my life could have been different? Yes, of course. But if I hadn't walked that path, I wouldn't be able to share the story and hopefully change some lives.

From There to Here

In my moments of solitude I discovered that I could control who stayed in my life. I thought I was wise. I had wisdom to a certain extent, but I still attracted men who were older than I was. (I noticed that everyone in my circle of friends followed this same pattern.) I had four relationships and labeled all of them. The first one I *grew to love*. The second one *I tried to love*. The third one I *fell in love with*. The fourth one *I wanted to love*. As a grown woman today, I know that *none of those relationships were healthy for me*. They all bruised me in some way.

I am my own worst critic. Sometimes it takes other people to hold the mirror up so you can see yourself. I decided at the age of 33 that I would remain single, especially since it seems that I have been in long-term relationships all my life. **Ouch!** I have held my head down long enough. **I am determined that if you don't treat me right from day one, then on day two you don't have to worry about me.** I will let go before I settle for less. I have been there and I am done with that. I will live in true love. I will love myself and others. I choose to be healthy and have only healthy relationships with people. I can't change the past, but I can help shape someone's future. I will stand up against domestic violence and child abuse. I will teach one and reach one as long as I can. I strive to empower families and our communities. I believe I entered into those past unhealthy relationships because I didn't love myself enough. I wanted love, but have yet to receive it in a form that is honorable in God's eyesight. To me, that means a husband, not a baby's daddy. I do not want any soul ties with ungodly men. I will remain as I am, single, celibate and free. I will know when my time has arrived. No longer can the whisperers whisper in my ear. For when you listen to the whisper, you make room for uncertainty.

When the brokenness heals, the bruise may remain to remind us that yet while we are bruised, we are not broken. When we are down there, there is nowhere to go but up!

Even as an adult, you may still have people who will try to knock you down. They may lie on you and even scandalize your name. As Donnie Mclurkin says, "After you have done all you can, you just stand." I have overcome obstacles and broken many barriers. I did not allow my past to keep me stuck. When you are determined to move forward and become productive, the impact shakes the world.

What I Have Learned From the Past

The first thing I learned is that the past is *behind you.* That is exactly why the rearview mirror is small. Take a small glimpse and keep it moving! Don't allow people to destroy who you are. When you are knocked down by life's circumstances, ain't nowhere to go but up! When you are already at your rock bottom, you have the power to bounce back up. I also learned a lot from the past that prepared me for my future. I learned that I have choices. My greatest challenge was staying down and my greatest victory was getting back up.

Through It All

I had to build up my self-esteem. If you allow what people say about you to strip your self-confidence, you have accepted the toxic think tank. Don't allow individuals who are poisonous to infect you. Remember, you are more than a conquerer, fearfully and wonderfully made. You are bruised, but not broken by the issues of life. You must believe in yourself, even when others do not. Falling, but still standing and pressing your way through. Throwing in the towel is not an option. Even a fighter who has been knocked out gets back up eventually. Love yourself, even if no one else does. I declare through it all to stand tall by standing up. There is no room at the bottom. The bottom is always crowded and the top is never full. Let your life message be a lesson for someone else. When a person is well, they have no need to pull down another. I know that through it all, I made the choice to be a part of the change.

Think About This

What words from your past have you allowed to dictate your life?

1. _____

2. _____

3. _____

How did your childhood experiences affect your life?

1. _____

2. _____

3. _____

Words and thoughts have power. The Bible states, *"That so a man thinketh, so is he."*

Keep your thoughts in line and your words in check. Guard your mind against negativity.

Move beyond anything that may hold back. Sometimes you may have to disassociate yourself from certain people. People can be like arithmetic. They can add to your life, subtract from your life, or even divide your life.

Simple Steps To Going Up

- **Pray** – Pray about everything.

- **Ask** – Ask for direction.

- **Clear** – Get a clear understanding of who you are.

- **Know** – It is important to know who can help you achieve things.

- **Plan** – Plan your life.

- **Dream** – Live your dreams

When I no longer accepted the ridicule, I accepted myself. I knew that I was somebody. Those same people who thought they could break my spirit are the same people who applaud me now. When people step on you and push you down, get on your knees and pray your way up! I asked God for wisdom and understanding and it was granted. I still have to fight my thoughts and misconceptions, but I always bounce up.

When you hit the bottom, remember, it gives you the power to go all the way back up!

"Pleasant words are as a honeycomb, sweet to the mind and healing to the body."— Proverbs 16: 24

This chapter is dedicated to all the girls and women who have survived the attacks of the enemy. You survived so that another may thrive. Shelley Morris stated it well when she said, **"I am a Soldier."** Do not back down. Take your rightful place and rise up!

Notes:

_____

_____

_____

_____

_____

_____

_____

_____

_____

_____

_____

_____

_____

_____

_____

_____

_____

_____

_____

_____

ABOUT THE AUTHOR

DR. TAMMIE R. MCCURRY

Dr. Tammie R. McCurry is President and CEO of Confidential Consultants LLC, a personal, professional, and relationship development company committed to educating, equipping, and empowering individuals within religious, social, and community organizations and corporations through creative seminars and workshops, counseling, and coaching.

She develops and conducts seminars and workshops that have been presented throughout the United States and abroad on topics such as diversity, healthy relationships, management, parenting, substance abuse education, and women's issues. She is certified by The Professional Woman Network as a Diversity Trainer. She is also certified by Life Innovations as a Marriage Enrichment Facilitator.

Dr. McCurry holds an Associate's Degree in Criminal Justice, a Bachelor's Degree in Social Science, a Master's Degree in Counseling, and a Doctor of Ministry Degree in Christian Counseling. She is also a licensed minister. Her knowledge of business and professionalism is supported by over 20 years of proven experience in the counseling, managerial, facilitating, administrative, quality assurance, training, and customer service areas.

She is the author of *Building The Unbreakable Bond* and co-author of *Silence*. An active member of the American Association of Christian Counselors and The Professional Woman Network, Dr. McCurry considers her greatest role and accomplishment as being a wife to her husband, Michael, and a mother to her six daughters, Brittney, Alyssa, Jasmine, Takia, Mikala, and Ashley.

Dr. McCurry is available to conduct seminars and workshops on a local, national, and international basis.

Contact:
Confidential Consultants LLC
P.O. Box 3795
Montgomery, AL 36109
(334) 649-2114
Email: confidentialconsultants@yahoo.com
Website: www.confidentialconsultants.net

TWELVE

GOD, CAN YOU HEAR ME?

By Dr. Tammie Ross McCurry

"For I know the plans I have for you," declares the Lord, "plans to prosper you and not to harm you, plans to give you hope and a future."
—Jeremiah 29:11 (NIV)

At some point in our lives, most of us have heard the above-mentioned scripture. However, when we are faced with the everyday challenges of life, we sometimes forget that God does have a plan for us. We find ourselves wondering if God even knows what is going on in our lives or if He even cares. Does He hear our silent cries?

Remember that time when you prayed diligently, asking God to give you a promotion on your job, but instead you got terminated? What about the time you asked God to let you have a child, yet year after year you watched your closest friends become mothers while you were still waiting? How about the exam you earnestly studied for and believed God would allow you to pass, but when you received your results…you had failed! What about the behaviorally-challenged child you have prayed for but you see no change in his behavior? How often have you prayed and asked God to "fix" your relationship, but it seems like your relationship has taken a turn for the worse? Is God listening to me at all? This may be the question pondering in your mind.

As women we face many challenges, disappointments, and discouragements in our lives. Sometimes the adversities of life will cause us to question whether or not God hears us when we talk to Him. I believe we must take a look at some key issues as we venture to examine this question:

- Do you believe in God?

- What are your motives for the request?

- Is your request in the will of God?

- Can you accept "no" as your answer?

Your Belief

In order for God to hear us, we must first believe that He exists. Ask yourself, do I honestly believe in God or do I just call on Him when I find myself in trouble? If there is no true relationship with God, how can we expect Him to hear our prayers? As children, many of us were taught to pray before we eat our meals, before going to bed at night, or when someone was sick. As we grew older, we may have continued in this same fashion, but did we honestly ever ask God into our hearts. Did we ever develop a true relationship with Him? Isaiah 59:1-2 explains it in these words, *"Surely the arm of the Lord is not too short to save, nor His ear too dull to hear. But your iniquities have separated you from your God: your sins have hidden His face from you, so that he will not hear."* In other words, if you do not believe in God and have not committed your life to Him, how can you expect Him to hear you when you pray?

When was the last time you actually examined your relationship with God? Do you really believe that God exists? Do you believe that He rewards those that seek Him? Or do you view God as some figment of your imagination? If you find that the latter is true for you, I would venture to say this may have some significant influence on why you may feel that God does not hear you when you talk to Him. Ask yourself this question, what are three things I really believe about God?

1. _____

2. _____

3. _____

As you look at what you have written down as your true beliefs about God, ask yourself another question: Do you really know God after all? If your answer is no, I encourage you to take a few minutes, invite God into your heart, take out your Bible and read Romans10:9-10. Once you have established a true relationship with God, it is important to determine what your motives are for your prayer requests.

Your Motives

Oftentimes, we have selfish motives for our requests and God may not honor such prayers. James 4:3 is very specific, *"When you ask, you do not receive, because you ask with wrong motives, that you may spend*

what you get on your pleasures." How often do you remember praying a
selfish prayer, one that would only benefit you? The fact is God wants
what is best for us. Remember, I told you previously that He has a plan
for our lives. However He does not want us to be self-absorbed and
self-centered in our prayer requests. How often do we pray to win the
lottery or make more money on our jobs? Are we praying this prayer
because we want to become debt free to be in a better position to help
others or are we praying this prayer because we want to have more
money so we can accumulate more things?

When was the last time you took a moment, forgot about your
own problems, and made a conscious effort to pray for the needs of a
family member or friend? Think back to a time when you have been
on the telephone with someone and they were telling you about their
problems, were you listening or were you waiting for them to take a
breath so you could tell them about your situation? We expect God
to listen to us, but most times when others talk to us, we just hear
them. There is a difference. Hearing is the act or process of perceiving
sounds, while listening is making a conscious effort to hear. Let me give
you an example, when we come into a room and our significant other
is watching television and we begin a conversation, how often do we
find ourselves asking the question, "Are you listening to me?" And the
response is usually, "Yes, I heard you!" On the other hand, how often
do we find ourselves attempting to listen to the children, cook dinner,
answer the phone, and listen to our spouses? Are we really listening?

God is not impressed by our selfish prayers. He wants us to be
concerned about the welfare of our family and friends. He wants us to
actually listen to their challenges and circumstances then come to Him
in prayer and petition for help on their behalf. When was the last time
you checked your motive for your prayer request? So now, you believe

in God and have developed a true relationship with Him. Your motives for your prayers are pure, but it still seems that God does not hear you. How is your heart?

Your Heart

Sometimes it is necessary for us to check the condition of our heart if it appears that our prayers are not being heard by God. Are we holding on to anger, malice, and unforgiveness? God cannot and will not honor our prayers when we have wickedness in our heart. You don't believe me? Well, let's take a look at what Psalms 66:18 says, *"If I regard wickedness in my heart, The Lord will not hear me."* It is vitally important that we acknowledge to God when we have angry or unforgiving feelings towards someone, then we must ask Him to remove these wicked feelings from our hearts.

Remember, it is not always necessary to acknowledge our feelings to the person we may feel has wronged us, but it is always necessary to acknowledge our feelings to God. He knows our heart and when we harbor negative feelings about others, it is not possible for God to forgive the sins we have committed against Him, nor is it possible for Him to hear our prayers. We must forgive those who hurt us so that we can come before God with a pure heart. When our heart is free of wicked thoughts and motives, we are better able to pray according to God's will. Take a moment and make a list of the people in your life that you know you need to forgive regardless of how long it has been, be honest with yourself, because God already knows your heart:

1. _____

2. _____

3. _____

4. _____

5. _____

His Will

How often do we make prayer requests that are not in the will of God? Let me give you a few examples:

- Praying for harm to come to our enemies

- Praying against our supervisors

- Praying against those in authority over us (i.e. our pastors, our governors, our president)

- Praying against our spouses

- Praying that God teach our children a lesson for misbehaving

We must always remember that God is a sovereign God. It is not His intent for us to wish evil or harm on others, even if they do evil or harm to us. In order for us to be in the will of God, we must honestly forgive those who harm us. This is a very difficult task, but it is not impossible, especially with the help of God.

When we find ourselves in prayer, we should make a conscious effort to pray for the protection of those who have attempted to harm us in any way. Sometimes we may find ourselves in a heated argument with our spouse or some other significant person in our life, and as a result, some very unpleasant thoughts may surface. It is vital that we do not wish them any harm, but instead pray blessings over them. This is an example of praying in the will of God.

Take a few moments and make a list below of some people you need to earnestly pray for that may have done harm to you at some point in your life:

1. _____

2. _____

3. _____

4. _____

5. _____

For the next thirty days, I encourage you to pray for the people you have listed. Remember to pray according to God's will. I guarantee you that God will hear you and will answer your prayers. Once you have prayed according to the will of God, you must be willing to accept His answer.

His Answer

Most times when we wonder if God hears us, it is not because we have not gotten an answer from Him; it is because we have not gotten the answer we desired. I believe one of the most difficult things for us to accept is when God's answer to us is "no" or "not yet." When we pray, we expect an immediate response from God. We look at the lives of others and wonder why God would answer their prayers but not hear ours. For example, think back to when you prayed and asked God to bless you with a husband, but yet you are still single. It could be that the right man has not come along yet and God wants to give you the best. Oftentimes, when God does not answer us right away, we take matters into our own hands and try to find our own mate. Then years later, what happens is that we find ourselves wondering why we are so unhappy in our relationship. Could it be that we assumed God's answer was "no" when it was really "not yet"?

How about the times we have prayed for God to give us a child, but we remain childless. Have you ever stopped to consider God's reasoning for not allowing you to become a mother at this particular season in your life? What about the child you were pregnant with but miscarried? Did God not hear your prayer or was there something that God saw down the road that He knew you would not be able to handle? Perhaps an illness, a genetic disease, a serious birth defect. Whatever the case, we must remember that God knows what is best for us.

I remember a time in my own life when I wanted a son so badly that I would pray daily asking God to bless my husband and me with a baby boy. Each time I became pregnant the pregnancy seemed to be different (the way I carried the baby, the way I felt) and I just knew this was God's way of letting me know that He had answered my prayers. I even had medical professionals to confirm through ultrasound their predictions of us having a son. However, as of the date of this publication, God's answer has remained "not yet." Please don't get me wrong. I am extremely thankful and proud to be the mother of my six daughters, because each of them is a blessing in her own unique way. But I still had this deep desire to have a son. I remember experiencing feelings of depression when my friends would give birth to baby boys and, although I was depressed and upset, God did not change His answer regarding this matter in my life. Even though we may be devastated, discouraged, and even torn apart on the inside when God does not grant our immediate request, we must realize that He is our father and just like with our own children, we do not always say "yes" to their requests. If we feel that what they are requesting will cause hurt, harm, or danger to them, we will take the risk of them having upset feelings towards us and tell them "no" because we know what is best for them. God loves us. He created us. Why would we think He wouldn't know what is best for us?

His Assurance

As we maintain our relationship with God, have pure motives for our prayers, examine our hearts to ensure there is no wickedness dwelling within us, and pray according to His will, He assures us that He will hear our prayers. Take a look at what 2 Chronicles 7:14 says, *"If my people which are called by my name, shall humble themselves, and pray, and seek my face, and turn from their wicked ways; then will I hear from heaven, and will forgive their sin, and will heal their land."* What an awesome assurance! If we can just give up our right to be right and humble ourselves regardless of the situation or circumstance, God assures us that He will hear us and answer our prayers. We began this chapter with a question – God, can you hear me? The answer is "yes," God does hear us. He may not answer the way we expect or in the time we expect, but He will always provide an answer for us. We must accept that although we want His answer to always be "yes" to our requests, He may answer with a simple "no" or "not yet." Nevertheless, He will answer us!

Recommended Reading

Comparative Study Bible, Zonderman Publishing, 1999.

ABOUT THE AUTHOR

BARBARA RICH

Barbara Rich is a highly skilled Insurance Sales Professional with over 25 years of specialized training and experience in Sales and Marketing. She is also involved in providing Sales and marketing Consulting and coaching for Individuals, small businesses and Home based businesses.

She has a strong passion to provide products and services that empower, strengthen and encourage women of all ages and backgrounds to achieve their life goals and dreams. One of her primary goals in life is to live out her God given purpose and to encourage others to do the same through their faith. She is a firm believer that if you keep God first and live by his principles, everything else in your life will fall into place.

THIRTEEN

10 STEPS TO A JOYOUS LIFE

By Barbara Rich

Are you a Christian woman who is tired of the mental, physical and emotional pressures that life brings? Do you wonder why do you feel that way if you are a Christian and supposed to be a daughter of the highest God? This chapter is written for YOU whether you are married, single, divorced, lonely, sick, broke or whatever your situation.

As the word says, *"Weeping may endure for a night, but joy comes in the morning."*—Psalm 30:5.

First, before we really get started, ask yourself what is joy and why do you need it? I define joy as happiness that is not based on your circumstances. In other words, regardless of your job situation, work, family, finances or relationships, you still have joy in your heart. Another way I like to define joy is **Jesus Over You**.

I believe that if you don't have inner joy, you will always be looking for something to fill that happiness void in your life. You could spend your entire life searching for it and you may never find it.

This chapter was inspired by a "joyless Christian." Now, you're probably wondering what is a joyless Christian? These are the people walking around with their heads down, feeling sorry for themselves, with critical spirits. Everyone is wrong but them, nothing is ever right, it's someone else's fault, and questioning why is this happening to me? Shall I go on? Now, don't get me wrong. I'm not saying that in spite of what is going on in your life you should always have a smile on your face.

In this life, you will have your share of pain and sorrow; you can count on that! Just keep living. I am talking about a general well-being and peace about your overall life in general. But if you continue to live your life waiting for things to get better based on your circumstances, I don't think you will ever really be truly happy. Why don't you end the search now and get along with living a truly joyous and happy life the way God meant you to live.

Now, let's get started and get our life set on the Joy track.
1.   Get out of your rut.

Get off the sofa and decide that this is the day the Lord has made and you shall rejoice and be glad and finally start making changes.

2.   Take care of yourself.

- Accept yourself as you are.

- Love yourself, the good, bad and ugly.

- Trust yourself and your instincts.

- Get your body in physical shape; exercise at least twice a week.

- Start with walking slowly, and then gradually build up your speed and time.

- Eat proper healthy foods.

- Make peace with anyone in your life who you are not talking to or getting along with.

- Be willing to forgive and let go of past hurts. (Remember, this is a requirement if you want your Father to forgive you.) Remember that today is the first day of the rest of your life and your time on this earth is not long. Also keep in mind that tomorrow is not promised to anyone.

*"A cheerful look brings joy to the heart,
and good news gives health to the bones."*—Proverbs 15:30

3. **Pray every day, once in the morning and again at night.**

- Get to know your Savior by reading his word daily.

- Remember, he loves you and wants to help you! He wants the best for you at all times.

- Bring all your problems and requests to him and leave them there.

- Pray for others.

- Learn to let go. I mean really let go. Give it to God and leave it there and don't take it back.

- Pray for your children, spouse and family members regularly.

- Pray with your spouse and children.

- Confess your sins regularly, ask for forgiveness, and don't do whatever again. Finally truly receive his forgiveness.

"Be joyful in hope, patient in affliction, faithful in prayer."
—Romans 12:12

4. Get your career in order.

It does not matter whether you are a stay-at-home mother, administrative assistant or corporate lawyer. Be the best you can without sacrificing your own personal life or family. Continue to learn and grow in your chosen profession. If you don't like your job, why don't you do something about it now? Take a class or start your own business. Do something you are passionate about. Don't just stay where you are, no matter what anyone says or what your wallet is telling you.

5. Get involved in a Christ-centered church.

Get to know your spiritual leaders well. Make sure your church is meeting all of your spiritual needs, such as programs for you, your spouse and your children that will really help you to grow in your spiritual life. Do not volunteer for everything, but volunteer for the things that can help others and that you are passionate about.

6. Keep your house clean.

De-clutter your house, car, desk, and closet. Let your children and spouse help by delegating jobs for them to handle and truly let them handle it. So what if that don't do it like you. They will learn and get better the more they do it. They will also appreciate that you showed them how to do things that will help them in their adult life. Remember, you are preparing your children to one day be on their own and not depend on you. That is the goal.

7. Be social and remember, to have a friend you have to be a friend.

Downsize the number of friends you have. Split your friends into acquaintances and actual real friends. Be careful who you let in your circle of friends. Don't hang around negative people. Don't let others bring or take you down. If they do, eliminate them from your life and do it quickly.

> *"The fruit of the spirit is love, joy, peace, patience, kindness, goodness, faithfulness, gentleness and self-control."*—Galatians 5:22-23

8. Be real and honest with yourself, others and more importantly, with God.

Search your heart. Is there anything in it that you need to let go? Do it now. Stop procrastinating. When you say you are going to do something, do it. Be a person of your word. Stop caring about what others think of you.

9. Get your finances in order.

Stop charging and overspending. It's just stuff. Live within your means. Tithe consistently. Stop using shopping as something to fill the void in your life.

"Consider it pure joy whenever you face trials of many kinds, because you know that the testing of your faith develops perseverance."—James 1:2,3

10. Talk to your spouse and children.

- Create a real relationship with them.

- Don't always criticize or give negative feedback.

- Try building up and encouraging instead of tearing them down.

- Let them make their own mistakes. Stop trying to save or change them. Let God do that. That is what He is there to do.

Finally, give all these items to the Lord one at a time until you have mastered them all. Change does not happen overnight. Start to enjoy everything in your life. Stop taking the small things for granted. Remember, all thinks work together for the good of those that love God. Love God with all your heart and soul.

Remember, the joy of the Lord is your strength and joy is not based upon circumstances. I guarantee that if you follow these steps, you will begin to get the joy back into your life and maintain it for a lifetime.

Respectfully submitted by a joyless Christian who changed!

Notes:

ABOUT THE AUTHOR

TALISA BEASLEY

A sought after speaker, certified life coach, author and consultant, Talisa Beasley is the founder of In the Beginning Consulting, a full service empowerment firm that serves as an educational and personal development consulting firm committed to strengthening families by empowering women and youth. Ms. Beasley is known as the "Benefits Coach" who seeks to help her clients become aware and increase their benefits so that their dreams move from fantasy to reality. She conducts workshops and seminars throughout the United States and abroad. She is best known for her contagious spirit and passionate delivery in her contact with her clients. She is a master at helping to facilitate change and goal achievement in the lives of her coaching clients, audiences and workshop participants.

An expert on Women's Issues, Ms. Beasley is a certified life and executive coach who has served hundreds of clients throughout the United States. Ms. Beasley is an active member of the American Association of Marriage and Family Therapists, Professional Women's Network, Professional Women's Speaker's Bureau, and The Atlanta Women's Network. She has received numerous nominations for awards and been selected by Metropolitan Who's Who as the New and Upcoming Professional.

A supporter of empowerment in body, soul, and spirit, Ms. Beasley is available to consult and keynote on a national and international basis.

Contact
In The Beginning Consulting
P.O. Box 48332
Atlanta, GA 30362
(404) 849-7544
Talisa@inthebeginningconsulting.com

FOURTEEN

HOW TO LIVE YOUR PASSION AND PURPOSE

By Talisa Beasley

"I've got a magic charm
That I keep up my sleeve,
I can walk the ocean floor
And never have to breathe.
Life doesn't frighten me at all."
—Maya Angelou

L adies, can we talk? Many women today are moving forward by great leaps and bounds. Today's woman is greatly advancing by becoming business owners, CEO's of major corporations, heads of state, and all without losing their stride as wives and mothers. However, with all of the advancement and prestige, women are still struggling in their lives more than ever. In a world where possibilities are endless, women are struggling with the idea of what they need to "*do*" instead of focusing of what they want to "*be*." As a result, women are struggling with such issues as low self-esteem, depression, and anxiety, among other things, at much higher levels than ever before. According to the Journal of the American Medical Association (1996), women suffer with depression and anxiety at twice the rate of men! This has got to stop!

It is my belief that women are doing only what is necessary to make it day by day. In addition, more and more women are appearing unfulfilled and are seeking more ways to find the purpose for their lives. I hear numerous women asking some of the following questions about their essence and purpose, "Why am I here?", "What is the purpose for my life?", "What am I missing?", or "How do I fulfill it?" I believe that the answers to these questions lie within ourselves and require taking a hard and thorough look at the bare essence of you! Now, I know what you are thinking. "Is this going to require me to add yet another chore in my life?" Actually, the answer is no! However, it may require you to change your view from what I need to *do* to how I need to *respond*. It is my belief that that each and every person is created with all of the tools needed to be a success. The key is to unlock your personal treasure and start living in the benefit of them!

With five proven keys of living your life with passion and purpose, you can begin to start living by using the resources you already possess. Let's change our conversation to talk about how to uncover your passion and purpose. Let's talk about a life that is full of achievements with such an impact that it can have an effect on you, your family and your community! Now, doesn't that sound great! So, are you ready to unlock your treasures? Are you ready to live your life by your own design instead of the design of others? So, grab some coffee and let's move into that life that you desire. The world is waiting for YOU!

Let me start by saying that I am aware that the woman of today have many responsibilities and the thought of taking on another task is out of the question! However, I would suggest to you that if you can discover your purpose and passion, all of your other tasks will lessen their weight, and ultimately will reduce your stress level. So, the question is, what does it take to live a life full of purpose and passion? Is it only available for some and not for others? Singer Mary J. Blige revealed in her interviews that early in her career she struggled to find her own peace and purpose in her life. She reported that she would watch singers like Beyonce and Alicia Keys, and admire their confidence and their ease in completing their tasks. She discussed that even though she was a rising star in the music industry, she often sought after the peace and the positive self-esteem for herself. She eventually found the peace that she sought and is now one of today's most celebrated recording artists in the industry.

Most of us can tell when someone is living with passion in their lives. They seem to put all their focus into whatever they do, and do not seem bothered about how much work is involved in accomplishing the goal. People with passion always appear enthusiastic about the smallest things. How does one achieve this feeling? I have discovered that passion is available for each and every person in life. However, I feel that many people are caught up with the day-to-day routines of life and trade in passion for money. Please understand that I am not suggesting that you not make money. However, I am suggesting that you can live in your purpose and continue to make money. I struggled with this as a young mother. I had so many responsibilities as a single parent that I put passion to the side to "handle my business." However, I have been fortunate to find my passion, and I would love to help you to find yours, too. I have found five keys that have proven positive in my life. Let's take a look those keys for you.

Key #1: Getting Back to Basics

Have you noticed that people tend to have a negative and distorted view of themselves? I have questioned this for some time. When questioned about why the negative view, the response is often a detoured answer that seeks to divert attention from self to focus on the external things that seem far less important. However, in order to be effective, the focus must be on the very core essence of you in order for you to handle the reality of the day. Steven Covey, the author of *Seven Habits of Highly Effective People* states, "Put first things first." He names this as the Principle of Personal Management. The goal is to develop a way to make your life congruent with your personal values, goals and mission. To further this thought, you will need to develop a mission statement for your life. Wikipedia defines a mission statement as a formal statement of purpose that guides direction. With a mission statement, you will begin to chart your life based on who you are and how you will live. You will be able to answer such questions as, "What do I want to do with my life?" or "What is my life goal?" Begin to recognize that you have a choice! Your choices will bring opportunities. Your opportunities will bring many chances for success! Take the time to discover your inner self. Your passion is bound to emanate from the core of your being to blossom into the fragrance that you desire.

Key #2: Switching Gears

My son's first car was a manual stick shift. You can only imagine how silly I looked giving him driving lesson with it. I should tell you that I have only driven a manual stick shift once, and that I clearly did not know what I was doing any better than he did. You will be happy to know that we, mostly me, easily burned out the clutch within two weeks. When I finally decided to swallow my pride and ask for help, a friend showed me how to properly operate the car. She informed me that I was to listen for the engine. As the engine revved up, I was to switch gears. Needless to say, I learned that my problem was listening. Unfortunately, we struggle with this every day in our lives. We ignore all the warning signs until it is too late and eventually something breaks down. Too many women I have encountered have said that they cannot change at this late stage in life. They feel that they had their chance and they are forced to suffer with the decisions that they have made. They say, "This is who I am." However, you need to know that it is never too late to switch gears, and that it is never too late to make a change for the better. There is freedom in knowing that you can make a choice to change gears whenever you decide. There's that word again, *choice*. Webster's Dictionary defines choice as "an alternative." You have the ability to pick the alternative. If you decide that you want to go back to school, choose the alternative. If you decide that you want to start a business instead of the dead-end job you go to every day, choose the alternative. Do you get the picture? Take the time to choose what is best for you in your life before you burn out your gears.

Key #3: Discover Your Flavor

Famous chef Justin Wilson, whose humor and Cajun cooking became famous in many American homes with such expressions as "I ga-ron-tee!" (guarantee). He was known for his flavorful Cajun food. When interviewed by the Associated Press in 1990, he gave this quote about his food, "Cajun cooking is the ability to take what you have, create a good dish and season it right."

When is the last time you paid attention to the flavor in your life? As we discussed earlier, life is full of opportunities. These opportunities allow for you to add the correct spices and the flavor you desire. As life unfolds, you discover what makes life good, what you can add to make it better, and the opportunity to try new things that add even a new hint of flavor. As I stated earlier, many are full of questions about the value of their lives. I believe that in order to find the answers to questions like these, you need to find out what sparks your "taste buds." For example, I know a woman who began her adult life as a stay-at-home mother. She stayed at home while her husband worked to support the family. When her child began school, she ventured out to get a job, and landed one with the local phone company as an operator. However, she soon realized that that was not what she wanted to do with her life. She eventually landed another job as a secretary for a real estate developer. As she continued to work in the job, the boss began to expose her to the world of real estate development and she developed a positive taste for it. As she continued to learn, her boss allowed her to handle more and more assignments outside of her normal job responsibilities. As time moved on, the boss developed a fatal illness and soon died. After the boss's death, the owners of the business talked to this woman about advancing and moving into her boss's position. She jumped at the opportunity! She advanced the company and eventually captured one of the largest real estate development deals in the city. She was such a success that she graced the cover of many famous magazines for her work in the real estate business.

The life that you desire is within your reach! The key is deciding to try different things to develop your own creative palate. As you move forward, you will revise and refine your passion. Pretty soon, you will also discover the common theme in your life, and determine how to hone in on it. Take the time to season your own life, to taste and enjoy the new dish that you have created with your life, piece by piece!

Key #4: Connecting to Greatness

Les Brown is a motivator for millions. According to Biography.com, "Brown's audience is wide: from Fortune 500 companies to automobile workers to prison inmates to special-education classes to ordinary individuals." Les Brown's message is, simply put, to connect with the greatness that lies within you to achieve the success you desire.

Have you ever considered that there is greatness on the inside of you? Yes, you have something so wonderful inside that it is screaming to come out. The optimal word to focus on is "connect." This requires you to take some action. Winston Churchill was quoted saying, "The price of greatness is responsibility." Previously, we discussed how to switch gears. All of these keys require your action. Focus on connecting yourself to the goal that you desire. I don't know about you, but when I am not connected to the goal, I tend to lose focus and never seem to complete my task. Eventually, I usually end up feeling disgusted and frustrated, only to stop the project all together. This is why connecting is essential to moving forward in your passion. Feel what it may be like to achieve the greatness. Focus on what it may take to achieve this greatness.

Michael Jordan discussed his feelings and thoughts he experienced as a young child, wanting to master the game of basketball. According to the National Basketball Association, Jordan struggled initially with the game of basketball. He did not even make his high school basketball team as a high school sophomore. However, this did not stop him. Jordan set his focus on his ability and the greatness that he knew was within him, and he worked daily to improve his skills. Michael Jordan eventually went on to make his high school basketball team the next year. Jordan went on to win several NBA championships, an Olympic medal, and various awards and accolades for his skill in the game.

Your greatness has yet to be discovered by you. One of the ways to find out your greatness is to try new projects that move you forward in the direction of your goals. However, greatness will never be discovered if you do not learn to exercise your gifts and talents. As you attempt the new projects, you will learn what you can do well and what needs work. As a result, mastery is created. Please do not be fooled by the word master in the word mastery. Mastery comes after several failed attempts. Thomas Edison stated, "I have not failed. I've just found 10,000 ways that won't work." However, Edison went on to create many of the inventions that we use today. Your mastery will provide you insight on your passion and your drive. Ultimately, your greatness will expose you to the course of change and innovation that moves you down the avenue of a fruitful future.

Key #5: Collect the Spoils

Living with positive benefits comes with a high cost. Now, I know that I stated that you would not have to add any further chores to your already long list of responsibilities. However, I want you to know that people who live with positive benefits pay by allowing change to come and alter their lives. The cost of change can be high. For this reason, many people shy away from change. Change means things will move from familiar to unfamiliar. Change also requires that you face the unknown with a bit of courage. This is what many of today's successful people deal with in their lives. However, they model the behavior of embracing change and enjoying the positive possibilities that it may bring. I call this collecting your spoils.

In ancient times, whenever a kingdom conquered another kingdom, there were always spoils to reap. Now think about it, the kingdom that won the war mainly conquered other cities to expand their territory and gain from the benefits of that new kingdom they conquered. This can be a model for life. Think of all the gifts and talents that you possess and the opportunities that lie ahead of you. You move forward, using the new abilities that you have discovered only to successfully move into kingdoms never known to you. As a result, you gain knowledge and the confidence to continue to move forward. Successful people are always looking for opportunities to sharpen their skills and move into new territories.

People like Microsoft Chairman Bill Gates are an example of someone who continues to master the skill of collecting spoils. He is a successful businessman and philanthropist who continues to move into new territories. Gates has ventured into the computer business through software design he and fellow college students developed that eventually grew into a successful business. As a result of this venture, Bill Gates became one of the wealthiest businessmen in the country. Gates continues to move forward by becoming one of the largest contributors to philanthropy. As a result, Gates continues to reap the benefits of creating new avenues that allow him to reap the benefits of change.

As you move forward to discovering your passion and purpose, you will find ways to focus how to increase your successes. The benefit of this key is to discover how you can use your newly found gifts and talents, and how they can benefit others around you. As you move into new areas of working within your passion, you gain a strength and confidence because things no longer seem tiring and stressful. Have you ever noticed how people continue to work without becoming tired? Those people have discovered their passion and can work tirelessly to accomplish their goal. In addition to working in your passion, you develop personal power. With personal power, your life begins to create a stableness that is no longer affected by outside situations. You develop a sense of a centered self that is not tied to a vocation or a company. You begin to direct your own life! You determine who you want to be and what direction you are headed. Now, that is power! Think of all that you could accomplish! Think of how powerful it would be to teach your children to master this skill. Low self-esteem in children would diminish, and we would be a society who raised emotionally strong children who would have the power to carry our society into the next generation. Now, that is a spoil that any kingdom would be happy to have.

Final Thoughts:

Steven Pavilna says, "Passion and purpose go hand in hand. When you discover your purpose, you will normally find it's something you are tremendously passionate about." This quote suggests the importance of getting to know you. Hopefully after reading this, you have decided to avoid living for someone else and take the reins of your life back. I hope that you have had the opportunity to get a chance to rediscover some things about yourself and bring back your passion. It is my goal to encourage you to reach for the sky in all that you do. Oh, and if you haven't noticed, I did not focus much on discovering your purpose. The reason for this is, if you discover your passion, purpose automatically will appear. For as you find your passion, you have moved into purpose.

Notes:

_____

_____

_____

_____

_____

_____

_____

_____

_____

_____

_____

_____

_____

_____

_____

_____

_____

_____

_____

_____

ABOUT THE AUTHOR

ANNTOINETTE M. MCKEE

Anntoinette M. McKee is President and CEO of International Institute for Leadership Development (IILD), an organization specializing in strategies for youth and woman empowerment through seminars, business consulting and corporate training. She is a member of Professional Woman Network. She is a highly sought-after and energetic keynote speaker and facilitator. Workshops and seminars conducted consist of topics such as Woman in Management, Avoiding Toxic Relationships, Self Esteem, Superwoman Syndrome, Emotional Wellness for Woman, Leadership for Woman, and Raising Healthy Families in an Unhealthy World. Anntoinette received training in youth development by the Department of Labor, and is a Nurturing Skills facilitator and certified by the Professional Woman's Network as a Professional diversity trainer with a focus on Woman's Issues and a member of The Professional Speakers Bureau.

Ms. McKee's knowledge of business and professionalism is supported by over 18 years of real world and leadership experience acquired by working with corporations, healthcare systems non-profits, real estate markets and international travels to Australia, Jamaica and South Africa.

Among her many accomplishments Ms. McKee has co-authored *Bruised But Not Broken and Raising Healthy Children in an Unhealthy World* released globally August 13, 2010. She holds a Bachelors of Science degree from University Wisconsin Milwaukee and a Masters in Divinity from Grace Theological Seminary in Loris South Carolina. Ms. McKee is a licensed and ordained minister in Milwaukee, Wisconsin.

Anntoinette McKee is dedicated to develop and motivate woman and youth to become strong professional leaders.

Contact:
International Institute for Leadership Development (IILD)
P.O. Box 170126
Glendale, Wisconsin 53217
(414) 915-1768
Email:intleadership@yahoo.com
www.iileadershipdevelopment.com

FIFTEEN

WELLNESS: MIND, BODY & SPIRIT

By Anntoinette McKee

"Now, may the God of peace sanctify you through and through and may your spirit soul and body be preserved sound and complete, blameless at the coming of our Lord Jesus Christ."—1 Thessalonians 5: 23

What is Wellness?

Merriam Webster defined wellness as "the quality or state of being healthy in body and mind, especially as the result of deliberate effort." Wellness is not just the absence of disease, but as a complete state of mental, physical, and spiritual well-being that allows for better quality of life. Anything that causes you DIS-EASE is not contributing to your wellness.

There are three elements that make up the foundation to your life journey to wellness: mind, body and spirit.

The Mind

The **Mind.** It's the most powerful tool man could have received from God. *"Finally, brethren, whatsoever things are true, whatsoever things are honest, whatsoever things are just, whatsoever things are pure, whatsoever things are lovely, whatsoever things are of good report; if there be any virtue, and if there be any praise, think on these things."*—Phil. 4:8. While completing my undergraduate degree, I recall a science professor speaking to the fact that brain researchers have found that thinking about a particular event produces the same pattern of activity in the brain as actually experiencing the event. Draw from the well of your mind by thinking about good things and use your imagination. Think and see yourself being at peace, nurtured, prospering and having joy. (Hey, the other alternative is to envision yourself sick, poor, depressed and sad. YOU CHOOSE.) Failure is a product of the mind. Never see yourself losing any battle. Even when people around you say, "I don't see you being able to do that," or your so-called friends say, "Your dreams are just too big," you tell all those folks that it's not for them to see you doing anything, but as long as YOU can see it happening, it will happen. Have a winning and a positive attitude about yourself. *"For as he thinks in his heart, so is he...."*—Proverbs 23:7. So, if you think you are a failure, then you are for that time. If you think you are successful, gorgeous, and intelligent, then YOU ARE.

Now some of you may be saying yes, all this positive talking is good, but I have been down for so long I can't seem to get myself back up. To you I say CHANGE YOUR MIND! Change your mind about it all. *"Be ye transformed by the renewing of your mind."*—Romans. 12:1-2

For years I was told I was too dark, too skinny and just overall not good enough. I began to ponder, too skinny and dark for whom? As a matter of fact, I started wondering why I was even thinking about what other people thought of me when those same people really meant nothing to me. I begin to seek the face of God and my perception of myself began to change. He said to me as I say to you, "Don't be discouraged, and create your new normal."

Strategies to Achieve Wellness of Mind

- Have faith in God.

- Start to love yourself for yourself.

- Believe in yourself.

- God does not want you to be unhappy just to keep somebody else happy.

- Forgive and let go of those that hurt you, not for them but for your personal growth and peace of mind.

- Don't have a problem with people that have a problem with you; that's not your problem.

- Don't spend all your time trying to win over your critics; just run your own race.

- Your destiny is not determined by your critics.

- Surround yourself with people that are of the same like mind. (Remember, two cannot walk together unless they agree and iron sharpens iron.)

- Encourage yourself all the time.

- Tap into your power of choice. Make informed, intelligent choices.

- Keep a journal and write your vision for your life.

- Continue to educate and empower yourself.

- Start each day with a positive thought.

- Rest and relax your mind and body.

- Laugh A LOT.

- Celebrate other people's victories.

- Find a mentor: someone that is doing what you see yourself doing. Be selective.

- The decisions you make today are your tomorrow's reality, so be in charge of your life and mind.

- VICTORY IS YOURS!

Embrace Your Body

As a child, I saw my grandmother work from sun up to sun down. She would make breakfast in the morning, can vegetables and fruit, prepare dinner, wash clothes, make cakes for the church, visit the sick and clean houses for other people, all while taking care of ten children and many grandchildren. Over the years I saw her posture become bent over and stooped. I never saw this great woman do anything for herself. Unfortunately, my grandmother, as well as many women, sacrifice their personal care and growth to their unmovable commitment to others. Helping others is something that we all should do and I believe in paying it forward, within reason. But how can we really take care of others without taking care of ourselves? Some of us give so much to our husband, children, careers and churches, and the list goes on. How can we continue to give so much of ourselves to others while neglecting our own bodies? We can't be effective or successful at taking care of others if we neglect to take care of ourselves.

The body is a magnificent communicator, and the body does not lie. I've seen people at the office and I can tell they are stressed or haven't slept in days just by looking at them. But still, when you ask them how they are doing, they say "great." The proper care of your body is essential to optimal health and longevity. It is more than okay to make yourself a priority. Yes, it's all right to have a spa day with your girl friends and okay to sit at home and rest for a few hours and do absolutely nothing.

If you ask any woman what is one thing she could change about herself, she would probably say her body or weight. Let me first say NO B-O-D-Y is perfect. Some of us struggle with being too fat or too skinny. We see television stars having babies and within two weeks their stomachs are firm, without stretch marks, and breasts are plump and no sagging in sight. Come on ladies, this is just not realistic so stop comparing the body God gave you to someone else's. Your body was made gracefully and uniquely by a superb God. So be uniquely you, a healthy you. From eating disorders like anorexia to over-eating, these can produce issues such as obesity. Problems with weight are prevalent amongst American woman and they're starting earlier and earlier. The Center of Disease Control and Prevention says that between 1980 and 2007, the number of obese children from the ages of six to nine tripled. And the World Health Organization reports childhood obesity is already epidemic in some areas and on the rise in others. An estimated 22 million children under five are estimated to be overweight worldwide. Recently, First Lady Michelle Obama launched the "Let's Move" campaign to end childhood obesity within a generation by engaging every sector impacting the health of children to achieve the national goal, and will provide schools, families and communities simple tools to help kids be more active, eat better, and get healthy. Let's just be honest, most Americans eat too much of the wrong foods and our children repeat the cycle. We must take control and be responsible for what we eat and drink. If you go to a restaurant, order food and you can't make out what's on your plate, DON'T EAT IT. Create a conscious effort to eat and drink healthier to gain optimal health. I notice the healthier food I eat, the more energy I have and the better I feel. I also get a more restful night sleep. Be informed about what you eat and where the food you are consuming is coming from. If you eat meat, ask the butcher where the meat was raised and if the meat was grain fed, antibiotic and cruelty free or grown another way. I know this seems like a lot to ask, but remember, your body is a temple and you should be selective in what goes in it.

Daily Food Servings

- Milk, yogurt and cheese group: 2-3 servings

- Meat, poultry, fish, dry beans, eggs, nuts group: 2-3 servings

- Fruit group: 2-4 servings

- Vegetable group: 3-5 servings

- Bread, cereal, rice, and pasta group: 6-11 servings

To help you prepare for optimal health, you can start by considering these general recommendations:

- *Eat natural, fresh foods.* Try to stay away from processed foods and additives; buy locally grown when possible.

- *Hydrate your body every day.* Drink pure, filtered water, bottled mineral water, or herbal teas. Aim to eliminate soda from your diet.

- *Exercise Regularly:* Walking, jogging, gardening, cycling and even stretching are great forms of exercise. Take the stairs instead of the elevator.

- *De-stress!* First things first. Stress can kill you! In 2004 I was working for a great organization 10 to12 hours a day and strangely enough, loving it. I was not eating properly and actually at times forgot to eat or go to the bathroom. I was consumed by getting things done for everyone but myself. As a director, I wore many hats—TOO MANY hats and none of them had my name on it. In October 2004, I started to experience black outs, anxiety, shortness of breath, heart palpitation, sweating profusely, and dramatic weight loss. I knew something was wrong. I was diagnosed with hyperthyroidism caused by a hereditary condition known as Graves Disease identified to be caused by over- production of the thyroid hormones, and in many cases severe stress. After treatment, my physician gave me 3 options:

    1. Change my circumstances.

    2. Change how I react to them.

    3. **Die.**

I decided I wanted to live and not die and if any of this sounds familiar, here are a few suggestions to reduce stress.

1. Make a brief list of your priorities, i.e. family, kids, me, work, hobbies etc. I would suggest to put "me" in front of everything else simply because if you are not happy or healthy, nobody else will be. Trust me.

2. Divide the things you have to do by the following order of importance.

    A. **Urgent and Important** (You have to take care of them NOW!)

    B. **Not Urgent, but Important** (Things like phone bills are important, but can wait.)

    C. **Urgent, but not Important** (These are things that are important to someone else, but not to you, but you have been asked to do them.)

    D. **Not Urgent and Not Important** (Needless to say, they go into the trash.)

This is a multi-step process accomplished a little at a time. You need to be able to recognize stress before you can reduce or eliminate it. Taking a thoughtful inventory of the stressors in your life is the best place to start.

Spiritual Wellness

"It is well. It is well with my soul" is a song I would hear my grandmother sing. As a child, I wondered what she was speaking about.

Now I know. Your spirit man is truly who you are. Now, some of you are asking, "What is my spirit man?" It's the small voice inside you that you refer to when you say, "I heard something in me say..." or "I had a feeling..." Our spirit is the only part of us that is directly connected to God. Imagine yourself sitting down in your room, going through so much. You cry, you pray, and cry some more, but still you feel nothing is happening to improve your situation. Until a small voice inside you says, "I'm here and I attend to your prayers." You get stronger, and stronger. Why? Because your spirit made a connection with God. He is tuned into you and your needs when you pray.

Prayer keeps you humble and your heart tender to the leading of God's spirit and enhances your ability to hear His voice. Prayer is the answer to all the questions you have in your life. Ask God to dwell among you daily. God will show you truth, and will give you discernment to those things you may not understand. Just ask him. *"Howbeit when he, the spirit of truth is come, he will guide you into all truth...."*—John 16:13. Feed your spirit with words of truth, comfort and wisdom. Yes, you may be in the mist of great trials and tests, but speak life to your situation. I am convinced that words are building blocks of your life.

You have the power to speak death or life into your own life. You, not your husband, children or parents have the right to speak death into your life unless you give them the right. Guard your life, which means watch who you are around. If people in your inner circle are filled with negativity, discord, or gossip, then you either need to get a new inner circle or tell them to get out of yours. Remember, iron sharpens iron. Your words first affect you before they affect someone else. Statements like, "You're never going to be anything. I hate you! You make me sick," are all words that tell more about you than the person you are speaking to. If you speak death about someone else, then that means there is death in you, which means you are hurt, scared, fearful, or just don't feel loved. What's in you will eventually come out.

I implore you, for the health, wealth and over all existence of you and your children, have healthy, life producing conversations. Proverbs 15:4 says, *"A wholesome tongue is a tree of life, but perverseness therein is a breach in the spirit."* If you are struggling, I ask you to believe in yourself. The curative is to speak the opposite of what is coming against you. If all you see coming against you is stress, confusion and poverty, speak peace, soundness of mind and wealth. Speak the opposite. Don't leave your happiness to someone else. Philippians 4:8 says, *"Finally, brethren, whatsoever things are true, whatsoever things are honest, whatsoever things are just, whatsoever things are pure, whatsoever things are lovely, whatsoever things are of good report; if there be any virtue, and if there be any praise, think on these things."*

I Confess

1. I know God cares for me.

2. I am the head and not the tail.

3. I am successful.

4. I believe in myself.

5. I will speak life.

6. I will have joy.

7. I am wealthy.

8. I am healthy.

9. I am more than a conqueror.

10. I believe today is a great day.

11. I will train my children greatness.

12. I will forgive those who hurt me.

13. I will pray daily.

14. I choose to be positive.

15. I HAVE THE VICTORY!

ABOUT THE AUTHOR

Irene C.R. Williams

Irene C.R. Williams is a wife, mother of two, grandmother of three, and is proud to be one of the earliest members of the Professional Woman Network (1993).

A finishing school valedictorian and [college] dropout, Ms. Williams ran the gamut of jobs, the earliest of which included amateur singing and radio soap character. Her last twenty years' professional experience ranged from clerical to administrative, associate to management, and small business owner. A voracious reader, she reads all kinds of genres but favors mystery thrillers and biography. She has been writing since ten years old and will continue this passion for as long as she is able. The audio book and voice over business beacon; soon she will be joining the organization.

Married to a retired US Navy disbursing officer, they celebrated their 21st anniversary in March, 2010.

A breast cancer survivor, Ms. Williams and her husband currently live in Texas. Both dog lovers, they are eternally grateful that two canine heads of household, Puti and Lucky, allow them to be part of their pack and environment.

Recent projects:

Co-author, A Journey Within: Self-Discovery for Women – Ch 12

Co-author, Living Your Vision and Purpose – Ch 7

Co-author, Becoming Your Own Best Friend – Ch 5

Co-author, The Self-Architect: Redesigning Your Life - Ch 11

Contact:
(210) 421-5905
beb_icrw@tmo.blackberry.net
bebotski221@yahoo.com

SIXTEEN

HANDLING THE STORM: HOW TO SURVIVE THE GREATEST HURTS

By Irene Williams

Hurt: To inflict bodily injury; to cause physical harm; to feel or suffer mental pain. Why do we allow bad memories to linger and enslave us? Why do we urge ourselves to push the envelope, so to speak, and hold the pain in our thoughts, in our heart, causing us to needlessly retain the scars? Why does emotional pain go deeper and last longer than physical pain? At times, why does it feel like no one in the world knows how deep, how insurmountable your pain is? Does the world even care? When one's heart is in anguish, one of two things happens. Either one stays inside the shell and nurses the pain, or pick up, dust off and decide to go on with life. How does one overcome pain when pride is crushed and there is nothing left of one's ego? How does one survive searing emotional pain?

I. I didn't know what it would feel to see my father after several years. As a passenger on a fully booked flight, I was not sure whether to pray for a tailwind or a headwind. Sleep was out of the question. Did I miss him? I had loved and hated my father for so long I wasn't sure that I wanted to see him at all. A lot of bruised ego was involved in the twelve years I had not seen him. It is now too late for discussions which, in the past, more often than not turned into heated arguments. Time ran out; I no longer had the chance to say I was sorry. The opportunity to hear his jokes and me laughing at them will never present itself again. Yet, receiving the call telling me he's gone did not come as a surprise. The little girl inside me screamed for another chance to be with him. The strength of the past was overwhelming. Through tears, I wished I could be with the Papa who, a long, long time ago, loved this little girl.

I was about eleven years old when my mother told me the reason why Papa was not coming home every night. She said that my father had a *mistress*. I didn't know what the word meant and I was determined to find out. I was told that she lived in another house rented by my father, and it wasn't far from where we lived. I went to that house and found to my dismay a woman – *the other woman* – who tried to make friends with me. I wanted her to look like a mean witch. But she didn't look like what I wanted her to look like. I heard she was a beautician. She always wore make-up, manicured nails, pedicured toenails, tight-fitting clothes, and most importantly, never ran out of money, which I wasn't sure came from my father. I resented that my father spent all his time with her. It got to the point that my mother and I would see him only one or two nights a week. My infrequent communication with my father consisted of, "I need some money for this school project," or, "I have two letters to mail to my pen pals," and his reply, "Let me see what

I can come up with... after mahjong." Sometimes, he did not give an answer at all.

In his final resting box I saw a face I didn't recognize. In that confining box, the face I saw did not at all resemble the husband my mother slaved for and the Papa I adored as a little child. A flood of memories came rushing at me. I wanted to cry in private but the tears came as I was saying, asking no one in particular, "Are you sure this is Papa?" Pointing to the face in the box, I said solemnly, "That is not him." How could this man be my father? He looked ancient, gaunt and his hair was long on both sides of his face. Papa did not let his hair grow more than what could cover his scalp. He preferred his hair very short, almost bald. Angry at the strangers who stared at me speechless, I tried silence and allowed the memories to consume me. I am not one prone to displaying extreme grief in public and I didn't want to change now.

Papa was very funny and witty. He cracked [corny] jokes and I laughed at all of them, even the ones I didn't understand. I allowed myself to remember his familiar smell as he held me close to him while he and Mama in late night darkness walked the few steps to the house from the street coming home from a movie. I always pretended to be asleep as we got off the jeepney*** so he would carry me through the darkness to our house, then to my bed. Since he always came home late, we had to go see the late movie. His choice of movies such as *The Ten Commandments*, The *Bridge on the River Kwai*, *The Old Man and the Sea* (he didn't like it and neither did I); Alfred Hitchcock's *Psycho* (he was amused and I covered my eyes through half the movie). He liked war movies and disliked westerns; he thought John Wayne was monosyllabic and boring; he didn't like musicals and comedies, except for Jerry Lewis in *The Nutty Professor*. I suspect the sheep dog the professor's character turned into had a lot to do with it. He loved boxing, especially when "Flash" Elorde* or Cassius Clay** fought. Papa liked marches and, surprisingly, waltzes even though I never saw him dance.

His desire to have a son was implicit. The question of whether he wished I were a son was always in my mind, one I was certain he could sense, but dismissed and ignored. As I looked at the face that did not look like the father I loved and hated, I realized the question would never be asked or answered.

During bad times, he made sure my mother felt his anger and every neighbor heard it. He always spoke with a loud voice. Except when he was with **her**. Good times meant he stayed a night and the following day, which was quite rare. But rare though they may be, they made my mother happy and a smile would stay on her face as long as he was within her sight or she could hear his voice while he socialized with neighbors. It was heaven to her when Papa took her to war movies and boxing matches.

My father graduated with bachelor's degrees in Arts, in Education, and in Law. During his lifetime, he was a college professor, a policeman, a businessman [while also] a jeepney driver, an appliance salesman, an auto mechanic, a gambler, and a security guard. An accident involving one of the vehicles we owned sent him to jail, unfortunately as a result of a novice legal defense. His best friend in Law School unsuccessfully defended him. His time in jail disqualified him from taking the Bar exams.

Papa took advantage, at times unfairly, of every opportunity he was given. And when there was no outsider to take advantage of, he sought it within the family. He had a never-ending appetite for money and a fervent desire to please the other woman. He callously told my mother to take care of their obligations since his income was needed by his other family. Some people mistook my mother to be the other woman, since my father practically lived at the "other" house. Then one day he received what he had wished for a long time. His mistress gave birth to a son. The next four years produced two more boys. His world complete, Papa realized he had the best of both worlds: a wife that made a living for the two of them, and a mistress, the "love of his life" and three sons. His utopian world was perfect.

My father and mother were married for 45 years. As the first 'westernized' nation in Southeast Asia, Filipinos are prone to copying the American way of life. When she was younger, my mother briefly entertained the illusion of divorce. But everyone knew her love for my father was immeasurable.

Papa married his mistress six months after my mother died. They were together also for 45 years. But then the fairy tale ended. She passed of a heart attack one year before he died of … what did Papa die of? No one around him seemed to know. A broken heart? Not likely. It seemed ironic that the ones who saw death come to claim my father reported that he saw *money* on the ground – some said a coin, others said a paper bill – bent down to pick it up, and was gone. The hospital emergency physician reported that he had no pulse and no brain activity when he was brought there. Nevertheless, they tried to resuscitate him, but life had already left my father. The little girl in me did not get to say goodbye.

*Gabriel "Flash" Elorde (March 25, 1935 – January 2, 1985) was a Filipino professional boxer. He is widely considered as one of the greatest Filipino boxers of all time, along with seven division world champion Manny Pacquiao and flyweight champion in the 1920s Pancho Villa.

Elorde, who had an 88-27-2 win-loss-draw card in a career that spanned more than a decade, failed in his fight against his own chain-smoking and threw in the towel almost two months before he turned 50. He died of lung cancer.

**Cassius Marcellus Clay, Jr., born January 17, 1942, in Louisville, Kentucky, is considered "the greatest of all time" boxer. His anger at whoever stole his bicycle at the age of twelve made him decide not to have anything stolen from him again, and asked a neighbor to teach him how to box. As a teenager, before he turned eighteen years old, he trained for and boxed in 108 fights. In 1960 he won the coveted Olympic Gold Medal and went on to win his first world title. After that win, he became a member of the Nation of Islam and changed his name from Cassius Clay to Muhammad Ali.

***Filipinos are known worldwide for their ability to improvise on and reproduce first world technology into forms more attainable, given limited financial resources. An example of this ability is the Philippine jeepney. The army jeeps left by the United States after the Second World War inspired the making of these vehicles. They are copies of army jeeps, resized and remodeled to accommodate commuting passengers numbering from 20 to 30 all in all.

I was an extremely naïve 22-year old when I got married the first time. He was one of my pen pals. When the secretary at the sales office where I worked told me that there was a 'foreigner' looking for me, not equipped with prescience, I greeted him with a big smile on my face. I still do not have the power to foresee as I feel I should. Thirty-five years after I made the fateful decision to give my daughter and me a **better** life, the act of forgiveness is long in coming. But this is not the whine you suspect it is.

II. The painful topic of [initiating and finalizing] my divorce came to mind and became a **must write** subject in this chapter. The topic? An act of ***extreme betrayal.*** By the attorney I hired to help with my divorce.

She was a friend, a college buddy, of my supervisor's at the time. Her friendship with my supervisor was the reason I was referred to her. She came highly recommended. She tooted her horn when I first met her and rightly so. She was an advocate for homeless and abused women in the city, and established a home for them. I was glad to have met her. Needless to say, one of the first things an attorney, or most attorneys for that matter, tells a prospective client are their fees, and it is made clear that nothing is done until the retainer is paid. There is no such thing as contingency basis in the world of litigation, or divorce for that matter.

The most crucial reason I ended the marriage was the safety of my daughter. This story is related in the PWP book *Living Your Vision and Purpose,* Chapter 7: **Success In Spite of It All.** The attorney suggested my first move should be to find a safe place for myself and my children. The children's ages at that time were 9 ½ and 1 ½ . Nothing less than their well being was of prime importance to me. I heeded any advice that pointed to keeping my children safe.

Throughout the lengthy preparation period, I specified repeatedly that I must have sole custody of my son and that I did not want anything from the marriage other than the car I was driving. She made me trust that she believed everything I said, and that there would be no problem with my request for sole custody. It was important to me that she believed me. The children and I left the state and sought shelter with an aunt of mine. One of the unfortunate things that happened was the short period of time I was told the children and I could stay (two weeks). Apparently, neither my aunt nor her husband believed I was telling the truth about what happened to my daughter. To them, I simply wanted to get out of the marriage. The other unfortunate event was losing the car I was driving. My then would be ex husband was determined to make life as impossible for me as he could, not realizing the children would also suffer. In his anger and humiliation, id, ego and superego were working overtime in his quest for revenge. Telephone calls to my lawyer that I could not afford were not returned.

The day before the [divorce] hearing, my attorney told me that I would have to 'tell the judge what happened in my own words,' since only my testimony would have impact. She told me she could not speak for me. Slowly and surely, I started feeling like I was alone at sea, swimming as hard as I could towards land, but was instead getting farther and farther from it.

On the morning of the hearing, I was a nervous wreck. I wondered how long the hearing was going to take, and I dreaded seeing **him.** I was **always scared of him**. Then the earth opened up beneath me. It came from nowhere and without warning. Five minutes before my case was called into the courtroom, my attorney told me that I *would have to agree to joint custody.* When asked why, she said that the judge would never give me sole custody since my son was born in that state, and the State would not give up its custody of the child. Furthermore, I did not have the income needed to take care of myself and my children. *"Besides,"* she added, *"joint custody in this state is in name only."* What about what he did to my daughter? The person who I trusted was on my side, the woman who built a shelter for homeless and abused women, looked me in the eyes and with a chilling, sarcastic smile said,

"You are by no means a saint. Do you think people believe you?" I realized then that if I had money and aggressively demanded what I wanted, I would not be hearing those cruel words from her. It all fell into place: the way she looked at me during the two meetings in her office was never with empathy. She looked at me with sarcasm; her attitude was of distrust and cynicism. She told me I was merely an ignorant mail-order bride who got tired of the game. The attorney I paid to protect me believed my husband's words instead. I felt utterly defeated. At that moment in time, I would not have felt any worse if the earth opened up and swallowed me. The time spent in front of the judge to me became a farce, an absurd travesty. It lasted less than fifteen minutes.

I filed a grievance against my attorney with the State Bar Association. My complaint was directed to the city I left, where she was practicing, and was forwarded to another attorney to investigate. As if I did not know how it would end, I received a letter telling me that the investigation resulted in her being found not in violation of any rule. My complaint was investigated and she was found innocent of all that I reported in my letter. The investigating entity – in an ironic twist – was the judge who swore me in during my citizenship ceremony.

So you see, this is not a whine about marriage. I am a believer of the institution of marriage, its sanctity and everything that it comes with. Preferably less of the *poorer* and *sickness,* and more of the *have and hold, trust, cherish,* maybe even *obey.* What God has joined together, let no man put asunder? According to the National Center for Health Statistics, the divorce rate rose from 2.5 per 1000 population in 1965 to 4.8 in 1975. 1975 had slightly better odds of reaching their tenth and fifteenth wedding anniversaries with their marriages still intact. I wonder what percentage of those divorces involved child [sexual] abuse. I wonder how many were never reported. Why involve innocent, vulnerable children? Is it genetic or chromosomal? XXY? XYY? The combination **must** be known **and revealed!** Is it a social disease?

III. Nowadays, my children don't talk to each other much. A hectic work schedule, an overwhelming career, a deteriorating union – these and every other reason or excuse can create a barrier and forget that the gap, the distance may grow wider and the bridge may become harder to build. I miss achingly the times when brother and sister were communicating, sometimes shouting at one another, but communicating, nevertheless. The man who sexually abused my daughter is my son's father? This is the first time I've put these words in print. I've thought it, I've said them, now I see them. This deep, deep pain never fails to crush my heart and bring tears to my eyes. I know I am not alone; still, I do not wish this on any parent. Now that I've seen the words I've dreaded, the words that have haunted me for so many years, that bore into my tortured soul and left my heart numb, I no longer desire to talk of it again. As I said earlier in this chapter, forgiveness is quite slow in coming. I feel pity, for the weight on his shoulders must be enormous. One can only hide the truth for so long. One can hide behind the façade of righteousness, but never forever.

Like my daughter, I, too, have moved on with my life. I hope and pray that she always finds herself in a good place. You see, I have survived! I have forgiven myself. I cast away shame and guilt in my suffering, in what I went through. I am a continual work in progress, forging ahead, not looking back. I am no longer my mistakes. The illusion of comfort in denial is no longer mine. There is no healing in silent self-torment. I own responsibility for baggage I have chosen to carry. I deserve the peace I have prayed for my children and myself. Empowered by acknowledgment, gratitude is now my virtue. Is there relief in recognition? I don't know. I do know I can let go of what no longer works. My heart is free to trust, to perceive, to judge or tell it like it is. I am in that "**one day**..." place: One day the pain will diminish, then disappear. And with head held high, get up and dust off. Life is too precious to waste on shame and guilt and torment. I am not in Kansas anymore!

ABOUT THE AUTHOR

SHANIKA HATCHER

Shanika Hatcher, BS, MS, QPP, CTIC., is the Executive Director of the First Samuel (W)Holistic Resource Center & Foundation Collection, Inc., she oversees the philanthropic team at First Samuel Church (W)Holistic Ministries, under the leadership of her pastor, Bishop Peter Fenton. Shanika is an author, motivational speaker, facilitator, writer, song writer, poet, drug & alcohol prevention specialist and philanthropic educator. She is the Foundation Collection director for the philanthropic library, located at First Samuel, and is currently leading the development of an adult literacy/ leadership and daycare library. She received her BS in Psychology and MS in Library & Information Science at Indiana University School of Library & Information Science. Shanika is a recent recipient of *Indiana's- Librarians Leading in Diversity,* Master's of Library Science (MLS) fellow, receiving a *Laura Bush 21ˢᵗ Century Librarian* Fellowship. For more information about Shanika's fellowship, please visit http://in.gov/library/3703. htm. Shanika's currently employed at the Indianapolis -Marion County Public Library for the past 15 years. Shanika's accomplishment includes two books: Co-author of *"Bruised but Not Broken"* & co-author of *"Raising a Healthy Child in an Unhealthy World."* She's a certified *Drug & Alcohol* Prevention Professional (QPP) and certified Teen Image Consultant (CTIC). She belongs to numerous professional and community organization to name a few: Association for Library & Information Science Grad Students IU SLIS (ALISS), Indiana Black Librarians Network (IBLN), Professional Woman Network (PWN), Indiana Healthy Marriage and Family Coalition, Inc. (IHMFC), American Library Association (ALA), Indiana Library Federation (ILF) and Common Concern for Youth Coalition, Inc. (CCYC). **Ms. Hatcher is a frequent featured facilitator, trainer and speaker on a variety of topics related to the education of philanthropy, youth development, and drugs & alcohol prevention:** How to approach a Foundation, Foundation *Grants to Nonprofits,* Proposal Writing, Foundation *Grants to Individuals* (scholarships, fellowships, and awards), Social Etiquette: Behavior for Specific Situations, How to Handle Situations When Bias & Prejudices is Directed at You and Self-Esteem Skills for Children & Teenager.

This chapter is dedicated to my daughter, Shanequia Marie Gill (Hatcher), who I gave birth to when I was twelve years old and my mother, Alice Marie Hatcher, who tried her best to raise me. I would also like to share a message sent from my spiritual father in the ministry, Bishop Peter Fenton, First Samuel Church (W)Holistic Ministries in Indianapolis, Indiana: "We are very thankful that God has allowed Shanika to share her life journey. Our prayer is that her testimony will impact lives. She is truly an example of a Woman of God and her life is proof that God is able to do all things—except fail!"

SEVENTEEN

THE PRINCESS WITHIN

By Shanika Hatcher

Genesis 17:5 states, *"And God said unto Abraham (Father of Many Nations), as for Sarai thy wife, thou shalt not call her name Sarai, but Sarah shall her name be."* Originally named Sarai, the Lord renamed her Sarah, meaning **princess**, after she had married Abraham. In Genesis 17:15-16 we read, *"And I will bless her, and give thee a son also of her: yea, I will bless her, and she shall be a mother of nations; kings of people shall be of her."* What does this tell us? You are royalty *(princess)* if you are a bride of Jesus Christ and the best is yet to come!

This chapter is dedicated to all young women that have been bruised, whether physically, sexually, psychologically or spiritually. The dictionary defines bruised as "abused, injured, or hurt slightly as with an insult or unkind remark." My prayer is that you will receive healing through the story of my pain, but most of all I hope that you are inspired by God's words that appear in this chapter.

The Bible tells us in Isaiah 53:4 that, *"Jesus hath borne our griefs and carried our sorrows."* The word "sorrows" (Hebrew – "makob") and griefs (Hebrew – "choli") refer to physical pain, sickness, and disease. However, as all Christians know, by Jesus stripes we are healed. The word "stripes" in Hebrew is "kawborah," which means to be black and blue. Our trials and tribulations leave numerous bruises, just as when our body receives a bruise and the capillaries under the skin are broken. The bruise colors our skin, leaving a mark. The "mark" left on our body is known in the Kingdom of God as our testimony. Romans 8:28 states, *"All things work together for the good of they that love the Lord and are called according to His purpose."* In other words, as difficult as it may be to understand, our **pain** has **purpose**!

God allows us, his children, to experience pain, hardship, disappointments and failure so that we can depend on Him and grow into the knowledge of who He is and what He expects, which helps us to realize how much He loves and cares for us. Unfortunately, some people never learn from their mistakes and continue to experience the wrath of God. However, others learn from their mistakes and use their mistakes as a ministry to help those who are spiritually weak or lost. Just as Jesus was rejected, many people will reject this message, as well. But I hope that by telling my story, I will enable readers to avoid this trap.

The Princess Within is the story of my life as a teen parent. You may wonder how a little girl becomes pregnant at such a young age. The answer is simply not having Godly supervision or Godly influences in one's life. While it is true that I went to church faithfully every Sunday with my mother or grandmother, the church of Jesus Christ was not in me. I went because I was forced to go. I never desired a personal relationship with Jesus Christ. As a child, my mother was always sick or working and my father was never around. The only time my father came around was during holidays, and he always came with excuses or unfulfilled promises, so I never looked forward to seeing him or spending time with him. I learned the hard way that a lack of biblical instruction and discipline creates lifelong problems, which inevitably will surface one way or another. My day came when I found out I was pregnant at the age of twelve.

When we don't raise our children according to God's plan and purpose, we give Satan unauthorized access to our children. I strongly believe we are supposed to raise our children as royalty. God commands parents to train up their children according to biblical principles. In my case, my mother left her children in the company of untrustworthy people, whether they were family members, friends or babysitters. Unfortunately, these untrustworthy people abused us in numerous ways. What people don't realize is that when children experience abuse of any form, they look for love and acceptance in all the wrong places. At the tender age of twelve, I was pregnant and afraid. I kept my pregnancy a secret for three months. As every mother knows, when a woman is pregnant she tends to experience mood swings, depression, loss of appetite, weight gain, nausea, and, of course, the pain of childbirth. Because of my secrecy, I developed severe depression, fear and low self-esteem. This was Satan's ultimate plan to put me in bondage. By the time I mustered the courage to tell my sister I was pregnant, Satan's mission was accomplished. He had access to my mind, body and emotions, which caused me to look for comfort in food and people. I was at a crossroads. I could either become a statistic, another lost soul, or I could turn my life around and use my pain to give my life purpose. With God's help, that is exactly what happened.

On December 28, 1990, I gave birth to my own beautiful princess, Shanequia Marie Hatcher-Gill. Now, after the intervening years, my daughter is my purpose. This young woman of God has brought so much joy and peace into my life. She is strong when I am weak. She is a prayer warrior and God has anointed her to speak life over dead situations. She is truly a gift from Heaven! Recently, Shanequia and I both graduated. She graduated from Avon High School, while I achieved a Master's Degree from the Indiana University School of Library and Information Science, graduating with high honors. To God be the glory! God truly has given my daughter and I victory over Satan's plan and purpose. With God's help, I was able to raise Shanequia properly so that she did not make the same mistake I made by becoming a teen mother. I firmly believe that the curse has been broken. Satan is a liar and there is no truth within him. I implore you to hear my story and allow God to turn whatever pain you may be experiencing into a life affirming victory.

My story is similar to the one told in the book of Esther, in which God used a girl to save the Jewish people from destruction. Esther's story relates a narrative of God's provision and providence through pain, persecution and a steadfast faith in God, ultimately bringing about deliverance for God's people through Esther's spiritual journey. It teaches an important lesson: Those who humble themselves before God, He will exalt them. However, those who exalt themselves, God will humble them. We can see this being illustrated in Esther 1:10-22, where God demotes Queen Vashti, who has exalted herself, but elevates Queen Esther, who has humbled herself before God. But Esther's story also ties in with what I have been referring to when I talk about the princess within. In the book of Esther, Satan wants Esther and her family to bow down to him, but she refuses, instead bowing down to the one true God. Her courage was an expression of her royalty— the princess within her. Think of it this way: Every young lady is an Esther ready to give spiritual birth. Our testimony allows us to give birth to those without hope in Christ Jesus or a better future. When people read or hear about how God has delivered us from Satan's trap, this gives them hope that God will do the same for them. Have you experienced hardship and then been delivered by God? Have you ever made a colossal mistake, but witnessed God transform that mistake into your ministry? Then you can truly understand my story and realize the true meaning of the good news embodied in the Gospel of Christ Jesus. My prayer is that my story will save you from a life of regret by striving to please God, not people. Just as Esther, who was Jewish, won the favor of the King and everyone in the king's presence, if you trust God and seek to please Him, God promises to make your enemies be at peace and bless you (Proverbs 16:7).

What follows is a series of suggestions and exercises that I hope will assist you in fully realizing your **Princess Within**. As a princess, you must take spiritual inventory of the sins of your heart.

First, please circle the "fruit of the flesh" that apply to your spiritual heart's condition:

- *Anger*: violence, explosive temper or lack of self-control

- *Pride*: excessively high opinion of oneself, disdainful behavior

- *Insecurity*: worried about what other people think, excessive people pleaser

- *Division*: rebellion, standing against others, disunion

- *Lust*: yearning or passion for ungodly things

- *Jealousy*: desiring to have what someone else has

- *Sanctimony*: false worship and praise

- *Selfish Ambition*: ungodly motives, not caring who gets hurt as long as you succeed

- *Condemnation*: haunted by past sin and failures

- *Strife*: conflict that has not been resolved

- *Resentment*: feelings of deep anger or hurt caused by "bad memories"

- *Fear*: Allowing false evidence to appear real (opposite of trusting God)

- *Heresy*: Holding on to beliefs that have no scriptural truth (spiritual abuse)

As one of God's princesses, each of us must guard our heart and desire the mind of Christ. When we accept Jesus Christ, God renews our mind by his Spirit, changing our hearts' desires. However, we must actively participate in the renewal process by mediating on his Word day and night. Christian meditation is a means of inner healing; meditation is essential for all born-again believers.

Below is a scriptural exercise that will teach you what to meditate on.
Philippians 4:8 – Meditation Exercise, please feel in the blank:

"Finally, brethren, whatsoever things are _____, whatsoever things are _____, whatsoever thing are _____, whatsoever things are _____, whatsoever things are _____, whatsoever things are of _____; if there be any _____, and if there be any praise, _____ on these things. God commands us to meditate to prevent and relieve stress, depression, and a host of other spiritual maladies that can hold us back. People who center their thoughts on the world and its things (position, power, recognition, honor, social standing, fame, money, wealth, property) will live for the world. Meditating on God's Word allows us to focus on Him and to rise above the false ambitions associated with engaging in worldly pursuits.

We should continually meditate on the Word of God, allowing the Word of guide our behavior, character and conversation. Here are some old sayings: What we think is what we become; where we have kept our minds is where we are; our thoughts shape our behavior and future; what we do is what we think.

Below are some Powerful Princess' Scriptures to meditate on:

Agape: John 3:16

_____

Angry: Ephesians 4:26-27

_____

Attitude: 1 Thessalonians 5:16

_____

Betrayal: Isaiah 54:10

_____

Bitterness: Matthew 5:23-24

Blessing: Genesis 12:2

Church Family: 1 Corinthians 12:25-27

Confidence: Proverbs 14:26

Decisions: Proverbs 16:9

Depression: Psalm 147:3

Disappointment: Romans 8:28

External Life: John 5:24

Failure: Psalm 37:23-24

Forgiveness: Matthews 6:14-15

God's Will: Psalm 37:23

Gossip: Proverbs 18:8

Humility: 2 Chronicles 7:14

Hurt: Matthews 5:11-12

Jealousy: James 3:16

Mistakes: Psalm 130:3-4

Overwhelmed: Psalm 38:4

Prayer: 1 Thessalonians 5:17

Second Coming of Christ: Luke 12:24

Success: Joshua 1:7

Temptation: 1 Corinthians 10:13

Victory: Romans 8:37

Wisdom: Psalm 111:10

Worry: Matthew 6:27

Princess Spiritual Inventory Exercise:

Take a moment to list your spiritual qualities and how you can use them to advance the Kingdom of God.

Spiritual Gifts, Talents & Skills	How can you use them for the KINGDOM?
Example: Prayer	Intercessor for those in leadership to love and lead according to Christ's biblical standards.

Now, make time to pray, fast and meditate so God can reveal to you the ways you can enhance your gifts, talents and skills. The gifts God has placed in you are not supposed to be abused, but rather are to be nurtured. That's why it's important to seek God through meditation for wisdom, knowledge and understanding before taking on assignments and projects. The only way for this exercise to be effective is for you to activate your faith. Faith gives us the strength to know God loves us and wants the very best for us as we face our daily challenges. God wants us to be assets in His kingdom, but we must do things his way.

1. Why do you think we must have faith to defeat Satan and all of his lies?

2. Why do you think God wants us to fulfill our purpose?

3. Why is operating in your gifts important?

4. What are the consequences of not operating in our gifts?

For many years, I was ashamed that I gave birth to my daughter at such a young age, her father was always in prison, and that I didn't grow up in a two-parent home. I was ashamed because my mom was always sick. When we are ashamed, we keep secrets that ultimately destroy us. Instead, heed my story and know that you are royalty! But also realize that the battle against Satan is truly a war, and that **Princess weaponry** is the *Word of God*. Jesus said, "Man does not live on bread alone, but on every word that comes from the mouth of God."—Matthew 4:4. Knowing and obeying God's Word protects us from being deceived by Satan's lies. Satan is a spirit and he uses spiritual weapons that we cannot see. However, if you are walking in the Spirit of God, God will reveal all of Satan's devices. Next, God will teach you how to resist Satan so he will flee, speak life over dead situations, pray, fast, study, meditate, and lay hands on the sick so they will recover; my mother's healing is a result of the Power of God. God is truly the Master Teacher! Now I'm not ashamed, but God working through me is shaming the devil! Now, it's time to put on the Armor of God, as a Princess. You must wear God's armor daily in order to defeat Satan.

God's Spiritual Clothing:

God's Spiritual Clothing	Know the Truth About...
Belt of Truth	Jesus is the Way, TRUTH, and Life.
Breastplate of Righteousness	You are made Righteous by the Blood of Christ ONLY.
Sandals of Peace	The peace you have, the world did not give you nor can the world take it away.
Shield of Faith	It's impossible to please God without Faith.
Helmet of Salvation	You must know YOU are SAVED and BLOOD bought; regardless of what you did or how people treat you.
Sword of the Spirit	WORD of GOD – which defeats and destroys Satan's plan and purpose for your life.

"Finally, be strong in the Lord and in His mighty power. Put on the full armor of God so that you can take your stand against the devil's schemes, for our struggles are not against flesh and blood, but against the rulers, against the authorities, against the powers of this dark world and against the spiritual forces of evil in the heavenly realms. Therefore, put on the full armor of God, so that when the day of evil comes, you may be able to stand your ground. Stand firm then, with the belt of truth buckled around your waist, with the breastplate of righteousness in place, and with your feet fitted with the readiness that comes from the gospel of peace. In addition to all this, take up the shield of faith, with which you can extinguish all the flaming arrows of the evil one. Take the helmet of salvation and the Sword of the Spirit, which is the Word of God." (Ephesians 6:10-17).

"Please know that a good name is more desirable than great riches; to be esteemed (by God) is better than silver or gold." (Proverbs 22:1).

A Prayer for You and for Me…

Heavenly Father, lift up my sister, your beloved princess. I pray you let her know the royal position she holds in your Kingdom. I pray you will forgive her sins and create in her a clean heart and mind so that she can partake of all of your rich benefits. I pray you allow your angels to protect her from all hurt, harm and danger. I pray specifically for protection against incidents, accidents, diseases, and mental illness. I pray that she would make her refuge in the shadow of your wings. I pray that you will let her know that her pain has purpose. I pray that you will turn her misery into an effective and powerful ministry. Remove her from all evil influences; protect her from every demonic attack. Let no weapon formed against her succeed. Dress her in the whole armor of God. Help her to walk in your ways. Help her prepare for what you have in store for her, because she is your Princess, and all of her privileges can no longer be denied. Lastly, let her know deep down in her spirit that she belongs to a royal priesthood, a holy nation, and that she has been separated and consecrated for her Royal Position in Your Kingdom. *In Jesus' Name.*

Notes:

_____

_____

_____

_____

_____

_____

_____

_____

_____

_____

_____

_____

_____

_____

_____

_____

_____

_____

_____

_____

_____

ABOUT THE AUTHOR

LINDA F. SAMUEL

Dr. Linda F. Samuel is a professional trainer and an Adjunct Professor. She facilitates education and training via workshops, conferences, and online. She is a licensed social worker (Georgia and South Carolina) and licensed minster, with over 20 years of professional experience prior to obtaining her PhD in Social Work (Clark Atlanta University, 2007). Dr. Samuel also holds a Master of Social Work from the University of South Carolina (1990), Graduate Certificate in Gerontology from the University of Georgia (2007), and a Bachelor in Social Welfare from Social Carolina State University (1983). Her areas of professional experience include work in the criminal justice system, child welfare system, alcohol/drug treatment system, public health network, and healthcare system.

She actively holds professional and personal expertise in the following areas: Social Work Practice with Individuals, Families, and Groups; Gerontology Curriculum Development, Social Work Administration; Minority Health Disparities Advocacy; Caregiver Support Groups; Rural Health Education, Religion/Spirituality Research; and Women Ministries Networks.

Dr. Samuel develops, conducts, and coordinates church conferences, leadership workshops, and spiritual retreats for women. Her passion is helping the "broken hearted" find restoration through her outreach ministry.

She is a member of the Greater Highway Church of Christ, Inc, National Association of Social Workers, and the Professional Women Network.

Contact
Dr. Linda F. Samuel
309 E. Morehead Street
Suite 734
Charlotte, NC 28202
(704) 910-6401
lfsamuel@gmail.com

EIGHTEEN

BOTTOM OF THE WELL: CLIMBING BACK UP

By Dr. Linda F. Samuel

Like the many Rain drops that fall from the sky,
So were her tears.
Tears of Sorrow,
Tears of Pain.
For she had known pain and suffering for a season.
A season of Sorrow,
A season of Pain.
But the Sun did shine
And the Rain did cease
And she was yet standing
Strong, Beautiful & Resilient.
Yes, Still Standing
Bruised but not Broken,
Praising God for His Enduring Power.

By choice, we are all survivors! This inspirational poem was written soon after I decided to climb back up from what I called my *Bottom of the Well* experience. You may ask, "What is a *Bottom of the Well* experience?" To me, a *Bottom of the Well* experience is a tragic heart wrenching life event filled with unbearable pain and suffering. It is personal and unique to each individual. For instance, imagine yourself experiencing the tragic death of a loved one, an act of violence, a sudden onset of an illness, and/or any other great loss. You encounter a devastating blow and find yourself falling into a dark cold place, the *Bottom of the Well*. You are in so much pain that you wonder if you will survive and find strength to climb back up out of that hole.

How do I know so much about pain, suffering, and survival? As a social worker and minister, I have seen so many people fight to survive their *Bottom of the Well* moments. I have also seen them climb back up one step at a time. I, too, have experienced a few of those moments. Just like many others, I chose to survive and, by the grace of God, I was able to climb back up.

When I was in my early forties, I had a life event that literally knocked me off my feet. I was a devoted Bible believing holy and sanctified preacher with a whole lot of "power." Life was wonderful for a woman like me, because I had confidence, health, love and support. Yes, I had embraced my mustard seed faith and I thought for sure that by the grace of God I could handle anything that came my way. I didn't see this coming. For personal reasons and respect for others who were involved, I do not share the intimate details about my most difficult *Bottom of the Well* experience. But I will tell you that it involved acts of betrayal, abuse, and violence.

There is never enough preparation for bad news and/or emotional tragedy. Prior to this heart-wrenching life event, I would awake and stand in the mirror to see a beautiful woman who was strong in her faith and very comfortable with her Christian lifestyle. This woman had endured many ups and downs in her life. She was a survivor who had encounter trials and tribulations victoriously. Yes, I loved me for the woman I had become. Now, life had dealt me a hand I wasn't prepared to play. I felt as though I was physically, emotionally, and spiritually knocked down. There I was down as low as any human being could get, struggling to get up. I had fallen into a deep dark well of defeat and despair. At the time, I didn't see how I was ever going to climb back up to the top. This was truly a test of my faith.

I often compare my story to a story I read in the Bible about the prophet Elijah and the widow woman of Zarephath (I Kings 17: 9-16). Similar to my experience and perhaps your experience too, things were bad for the widow woman. There was famine and drought in the land. So when Elijah arrived at Zarephath, he found the woman gathering two sticks so that she could prepare the very last meal for herself and her son before they died. All she had was a little meal at the bottom of a barrel. Elijah offered her hope and told her to prepare a meal for him first and then prepare a meal for her and her son. He also told her that if she was obedient to the word of God, the barrel of meal would not become empty until the day the Lord sent rain upon the earth. She followed his instructions and she, the prophet, and her son ate for many days afterward. You see, although things were bad for her and her son, she received hope through the word of God and she increased her faith. I like to say that she found faith as she began to trust God while she was scraping the bottom of the barrel. In order words, she had "Faith at the Bottom of the Barrel."

How can we believe in something we do not see? According to Hebrews 11:1, *"Now faith is the substance of things hoped for, the evidence of things not seen."* We have to look beyond the situation and see a positive outcome. Hope that is seen is not hope. We believe that we can climb back up out of the well, although we do not see the natural way out.

For many of us, it is a constant struggle to find a way to climb back up out of at deep dark place. But we must begin to think like the man in the Bible who lay at the pool of Bethesda (John 5: 1-15). He had no other place to go but up. This man had been sick for thirty eight years with an infirmity that had him bedridden. He often visited the pool because at a certain season or time the Angel of the Lord would come and trouble the water so that whoever stepped into the pool first was made whole and healed from their condition. You may ask what this has to with a *Bottom of the Well* experience. The man was down and in despair, but he had faith that if he made it to the pool, he would be healed. He had faith and he chose to survive until things got better.

The man continued to return to the pool because he knew that one day he would be able to rise above his physical condition and live a "normal life." One day, Jesus came to the pool and began to have a conversation with the man. Jesus asked him if he wanted to be made whole. In other words, Jesus asked him if he was tired of being "down." By faith, the man was able to rise, take up his bed and walk. This was a powerful and inspirational story. This man was not only able to "get up," but he was also able to pick up the one item that had supported him for thirty-eight years, his bed. Yes, that's powerful. No doubt, this was a *Bottom of the Well* experience.

In conclusion, at some point in life we may find ourselves in a dark cold place (well). When trouble, tragedy, and/or heartache come into our lives, it is a difficult time. Life may seem shattered and hopeless because the pain and suffering appears unbearable. Although things may be difficult and hard, we choose to survive because we know that trouble and suffering makes us strong. Therefore, we must find the strength inside to climb back up out of that dark place one step at a time. We do so by identifying the steps we must climb to reach the top: *Acceptance, Faith, Love, Strength, Wisdom, Peace, and Joy.*

Seven Steps: Climbing Back Up!

Acceptance

- Evaluate your surroundings.

- Acknowledge that you may need help.

- Identify the condition for what it really is.

- Examine how you landed in this position.

- Accept the truth by examining your contribution to the situation.

Faith

- Be faithful to what you believe to be true.

- Accept your purpose for being in this position.

- Be authentic and true to yourself.

- Look up and see beyond your natural vision.

- Search for a new beginning and believe that the outcome will be positive.

Love
- Identify and accept your uniqueness.
- Embrace your inside beauty.
- Be original and creative.
- Encourage yourself in a positive manner.
- Accept that you are worthy of love from yourself and others.

Strength
- Identify things that you do well.
- Evaluate your weaknesses.
- Learn new ways to cope.
- Adopt a lifestyle that will break the "strongholds" in your life.
- Accept and use the power within.

Wisdom
- Learn from your life experiences.
- Refuse to find yourself in the same negative situation twice.
- Develop and embrace positive life strategies.
- Share your knowledge with others.
- Practice what you preach.

Peace

- Learn to relax and meditate daily.

- Adopt the philosophy that it is "well with your soul."

- Be faithful to yourself and the "cause" that you believe in.

- Be at peace with yourself and your GOD.

- Learn to forgive yourself and others.

Joy

- Accept and express your true emotions.

- Give equal time to work and play.

- Know and embrace your purpose in life.

- Celebrate your victory.

- Live life to the fullest each day.

Seven Steps: Climbing Back Up Worksheet

1. Define your well.
   a. Describe the situation.

   _____

   _____

   b. Identify individuals involved.

   _____

   _____

2. Describe your surroundings.

_____

_____

_____

3. List your strengths and weaknesses.

_____

_____

_____

_____

4. Develop your strategy: List your resources.

_____

_____

_____

5. Write down the key components of your "Faith."
    a. Describe your calm place.

_____

_____

    b. List the tools you will use to sharpen your "Faith."

_____

_____

6. Describe how you plan to climb up.
    a. Identify your support system.

_____

_____

_____

7. Record how you plan to celebrate your victory!
   a. Record positive affirmations.

   _____

   _____

   _____

   b. List ways you plan to celebrate life at the top of the well.

   _____

   _____

   _____

   _____

   May your journey upward be blessed.

ABOUT THE AUTHOR

BRENDA LEWIS

I was born and raised in Milwaukee, WI by my mother who was single. We didn't have much but we made it through a lot of trials and tribulation. I have been able to overcome a 14 year battle of cancer only to see my mom lose to that same battle. I graduated from high school with high honors and went on to college. Due to the loss of both my mother and my 1month old son only six months apart, I was forced to take a break from college in my last semester. What I thought would be the end was only the beginning.

God led me to start my own business back in September 1996, it was called Serenity Christian learning center. As the vision grew so did we and in 2003 we changed locations and the name to Open Arms Academy; a program designed to teach both normal and special needs children. However, God was not through with me or the vision. In August of 2009 we were blessed with a new location and a extension on the vision. Our program was now called Imagine me Being me LLC. This program was designed to not only help children but young teenage parents, special needs children and young adults. It has designed a housing program for those who are participating in the program and an awesome educational program for our young and gifted children.

It wasn't until this past March that God led me to put the finishing touches on such a program. We are now "The Imagine Me International Institute." I am President/CEO of this great organization, and we are going international with this vision.

Education: North Division High School
University of Wisconsin-Milwaukee
Achievements:

I am President/CEO of numerous companies that fall under the umbrella of the institute. I am a mentor for teenage girls/young women. I am a great mother of a special needs child whom I was bless to adopt. I am an International author of two books: "Raising Healthy Children in an Unhealthy World" and "Bruised But Not Broken".

I believe that life is what you make of it, so work hard and go strong and you will succeed!!!

Contact:
Jacksonopenarms@aol.com

NINETEEN

LIVING WITH CHRONIC ILLNESS

By Brenda Lewis

In the Bible it talks about how God will never put more on you then you can bear. (Well, at least that's what my mother use to say.) I wondered if she still believed that after she was diagnosis with a brain tumor at the age of 35 years old. I believe that was the day her world changed forever. I was about 12 years old when I came home from school and saw my mom in her room down on her knees praying. I remember her asking God to please heal her and if it was not His will, to heal her at least until all her children were grown and graduated from high school. It was the first time I challenged God to prove that he really existed. (I know you may not agree with me doing that, but this was my mom and she trusted God and I wanted to see why.)

I can't tell you what happened with the brain tumor because my mom was very secretive with her health issues. I can tell you that for about seven years my mom was doing great and living life to the fullest.

When my mom turned 42 years old, her health began to decline terribly. She was diagnosed with kidney stones and needed surgery to have them removed. A year later she had another surgery to have her right ovary removed and one year later she had the other ovary removed in addition to her left fallopian tube. That last surgery changed all our lives forever because when the doctors went in to remove the tube, they discovered that my mom had cancer throughout her body. It turned out that the cancer had come back, but this time it was on all her reproductive organs. Every time they cut her open to do another surgery, to me it seemed like the cancer would spread to another location–fast. Due to such an aggressive form of cancer, my sisters, brother and I lost our mother to cancer on April 5th, 1995. We had one week to spend with her after we were notified about the diagnosis and I thought that was the most difficult time of my life, but I would learn differently.

I was 22years old when my mom died and it was difficult. However, needless to say, my life got even more difficult after a routine visit to the doctor. You see, I had a son and I knew I didn't want any more kids, so I was on the pill. When my doctor came back into my room, he said my PAP came back abnormal and they were going to have to do a few more tests. I had no clue what this doctor was about to say to me, nor did I know how serious this was because I had never experienced it. After more tests, he came back into the room and told me that they had found cancer cells on my cervix and that they needed to remove them at once. I was scared to death, being that we had just buried my mom from cancer, so I began to ask him how this happened and how were they going to remove them? Well ladies, I don't know how many of you read the little slip that comes in your container of birth control pills, but in some there is a disclaimer on there that says it may cause cancer cells to appear on the cervix. I would have never gone on the pill if I had known this ahead of time, but it was too late now. I had to have a small procedure where they froze the cervix and scraped it. I was fine for the next four years, and yes I got off those pills immediately.

In the early fall of 2000, I had just celebrated my 26th birthday and the following day I got really sick. I thought it was from all the celebrating, but I was wrong. I went to the doctor and found out that I had uterine cancer. My life had come to an end and I really didn't know what to say or do. All I could think about was my mom and my son and how I was going to make it through such a tragedy. I felt empty inside and as I looked up at my doctor, I saw he was crying and I began to cry, as well. You see, my doctor was also my mother's doctor and he took her death so hard. I remember he broke down at her wake because he never wanted her to have all those surgeries. I remembered him giving me a big hug and saying how we were going to get through this together and he would not let me die. You know, a lot of doctors would have immediately advised me to get a hysterectomy, but that was not the route my doctor was going to take with me. He had been down that road with my mother and he was not about to take me down the same path because he knew where it would end. I told him I trusted him and I would comply with everything he told me to do. And so began our journey.

He started me out on a very aggressive schedule of chemotherapy and created a special diet for me, as well. I had just started a new business and between the treatments and the new business, it just didn't seem like I was going to make it. I had my son to attend to as well and with such aggressive treatments, I had no energy to do even the little things like cook. It looked like a lost cause for me, not to mention that no one in my family even knew the things that I was going through because I kept it a secret from them. So who could I call on? I recalled a night when it was just me at home, as my son had stayed the night at his father's house. I had completed a treatment and I was so sick. My doctor brought me home that day and made sure I had everything I needed before he left. I fell asleep quickly because the treatments were so draining. In my sleep, I could feel my breathing getting shallower until I was awakened by coughing and gasping for air. My pain had become so unbearable that I could barely breathe.

As things became faint around me, I remembered when I saw my mom praying on her knees to God asking him to heal her. It was from that thought that I drew strength and began to call out God's name. "Jesus, Jesus, Jesus. I need you Jesus. I need your touch right now Jesus. I need you to heal me Jesus. Please don't leave me Jesus." I started crying because I thought I was never going to see my son again. I thought I was about to die. However, I kept calling God's name, just like I saw my mom did in the past. "Jesus, Jesus, Jesus, you are the keeper of my soul and I love you Jesus. Please don't leave me Jesus. Lord, I love you and I need you. Please hear my cry and answer me Jesus. Please Jesus, I need a touch from you." As time went on, I could hear my cry getting louder and louder until I was yelling out, "JESUS, JESUS, and JESUS!!!" Before I knew it, my pain had become just a small pinch in the lower part of my stomach and I knew I would be ok.

You know, when we are young we don't ever consider that the things that we see as a child could help us in our future as a adult, but in my case, I did just that. I really believe that if God had not bought back such a memory, I may have taken my last breath that night. (To God be the glory!) Night times were not always the rough times for me, but it was during the day that I really struggled. You see, I was hiding this illness from everyone and it took a lot of work. My hair started falling out from the treatments and so I cut my hair off to keep everyone from questioning me. (However, they still did because I had long hair so they wanted to know why I had cut it.) I use to tell people it was because I was tired of looking like a little girl when the truth of the matter was, the chemo treatments were taking it out. There were also times when people would ask me why I was getting sick a lot and I use to say, oh because of the stress of starting a new business and that it can get a little over- whelming sometimes. It never occurred to me that this could have been an opportunity for me to share my secret and get some support while I went through such a hard time in my life. I had to learn the hard way about how to get through this with the help and support of others.

I had gone through the journey as my mom when it came to treating this disease. The only difference was, I wouldn't allow them to cut on me. In 2003, I finally went into remission. I got married and I got pregnant. I was five months into my pregnancy when my cancer came out of remission and, sad to say, I lost the baby. In 2006 I divorced and my cancer went back into remission. After my divorce, I took time to recover from all of the drama and reevaluate my life. I needed to understand why I was going through such a horrible trial and why it was lasting so long. Well, my cancer stayed in remission another three years and during that time, we buried my mother's sister due to cancer (another scary and challenging moment), and once again her children knew nothing about her illness and they had one month with her before she passed away. I began to see the pattern of selfishness on our mother's part. They may have thought they were doing us a favor by not telling us, but really we felt cheated out of time we could have spent with them. I began to see that I was repeating the cycle, so I had to do something about it. My cancer came out of remission December 2008 and we buried my aunt February 2009. I decided to take a stand and come clean about my condition, so I contacted my sisters first and told them what was going on with me and how long I had been dealing with it. We cried, but I must tell you, it was a weight lifted off my shoulders. I then gave a call to my mom's brother (my favorite uncle) and told him and his wife and before long, the news had spread throughout the family. My family was definitely concerned and they stepped right in to help me with everything I needed help with. That helped me so much that words can't even begin to explain it! I finally had help caring such a heavy load. Nine months later, I was in Bible study and I was so overwhelmed with conviction of not trusting my church family that I was compelled to confess my secret. I told the members about my cancer and how long I had been dealing with it. I shared that at certain times I was ready to give up, but it was the word of God that was brought forth within the walls of that building that gave me strength to move on. (Lord, thank you for sending me to such a spirit-filled church. I would never had made it without them.) Upon completion of my testimony, I felt ok with having this illness and I was ready for God to use me as He chose. I no longer wanted to fight against God any more, so I finally let it all go and decided to let God.

Well, the day before Thanksgiving, I had made it home and just decided I wouldn't open any mail. I was just going to go to bed, because it had been a long two weeks for me. You see, what I didn't tell you was that prior to all this, I was seven months pregnant with my baby girl Nevaeh and I was excited. However, Nevaeh didn't make it into this world alive because the cancer in my uterus formed a mass that outgrew her and she died in my womb. Yes, I was devastated, but I knew and believed that God knew what He was doing and I prayed for strength to get through it all. Fast forwarding to Thanksgiving day, I woke up and decided to read my mail before preparing to go to the family house. Well, there was a letter from my doctor and I just knew it was a bill, so of course my whole demeanor changed for the worse. I opened it and begin to read, and as I read, I began to cry, because the letter had stated that she was pleased to announce to me that there was no more cancer within my body. I cried tears of joy because I was healed, but also tears of sadness because I believed that baby Nevaeh was my little miracle and had come and served her purpose. (I still miss you baby girl.) I can proudly say today that I am still cancer free and I praise God for the healing.

I was humbled and learned to accept the will of the Lord for my life. Once I became open and honest with my friends and family about what was happening with me, it was then that God was able to begin to move in my life on my behalf. How many times have we missed that observation? God is not the author of confusion and when we are running around trying to fix things ourselves, we only create chaos for ourselves. We have to learn how to stand still and seek God's face in the midst of all our chaos. Little do we know Him standing right by our side in the midst of it all, waiting on us to pass Him the flame so He can lead us out of our madness.

We often fail terribly when it comes to trusting God, and yet we still call on Him for His help. Sisters, we can't be delivered from others until we are delivered from ourselves. It is then that we will be set free from whatever (or whomever) has a chain on us. Remember, there is nothing too hard for God and I know and believe that with all my heart. I pray that you all learn this for yourself. If you live with chronic illness, please keep the faith–always.

ABOUT THE AUTHOR

Tamika D. Montgomery

Tamika Montgomery is the President and CEO of MTI Group LLC a Real-estate investment company in Canton, MI. She is also an Account Executive for Sprint Nextel Corporation. She is the wife of Michael Montgomery and Mother of 2- Michael and Taylor. She is passionate about people and good customer service and she is dedicated to helping Women improve their lives and achieve their personal and professional goals.

- Certified Coach by PWN
- A member of Prince Hall Affiliation Order of the Eastern Stars.
- A Reading Corp Volunteer for the Detroit Public School System
- Certified Residential Appraiser for the state of Michigan
- She is also a volunteer/member of the Multicultural Committee of Canton, MI.

Tamika dedicates this to her Husband who supports her 1000 percent no matter what! He's her best friend; and confidant he's her all! She also credits her Mother, who motivates her she was a strong woman who despite her Epilepsy and Asthma she let nothing hold her back from fulfilling her dreams and she always did it with a smile!

Contact:
MTI Group LLC
PO Box 87441
Canton, MI 48187
810.217.6122
ladyt1220@gmail.com

TWENTY

OVERCOMING DEBT AND FINANCIAL STRUGGLES

By Tamika Montgomery

I imagine you have always tried to be a responsible adult when it came to money and credit. Ever since you can remember, you attempted to pay your bills on time and were an advocate for having good credit. You learned about your credit score and what it would take to increase your FICO numbers and go to a higher credit level.

Well, that was me! Next level indeed! We purchased our first house at the age of twenty five and, though that may not have the "Wow Factor," for me it meant security. This house would keep my family safe and sound; we would call it home. I would do it in a heartbeat and wouldn't blink, but little did I know what would happen in the future to destroy this dream come true.

In 2003, my husband and I decided that we wanted to start our own business, something that we could pass on to our children one day. We came across an opportunity that allowed us to get into investing in car sales, so I called and made an appointment. When we arrived we learned that the program had been scrapped. However, there was another opportunity in its place! We learned that the real estate business was booming! It was a great time to buy low, renovate, and rent or sell high. It was so simple that we thought something had to be wrong! We had never thought about real estate investing, but we thought, "Why not?" We bought our first 'investment house' and were approved for several more. (The great news was that one property already had a tenant who was paying rent every month!) We set out to learn all that we could about real estate investing and talked with everyone we met who could help us reach our investment goals. We read all the books and watched every real estate show on television. We just knew this would set us on the path to **financial wealth and freedom, debt-free and retired at age 50!** We were going to be the next Donald Trump!

We were going to buy low, renovate and rent! We assembled a team and were on the ride of our lives. We were so serious about this that I even went to school and received my Residential Appraisal License. Our evenings were spent looking for more houses with the kids in tow and eating lots of fast food. Then everything started to snowball as we bought another and then another until we owned eight properties! It was like they were just handing them to us – it was too easy! (We even had our family and friends coming to us for consultation, as if we were the Gurus of it all!) But then IT happened. The bottom dropped out of our world.

During 2007-2008, sub-prime lenders were dropping like flies. What they didn't know (and we didn't expect) were ***Career Tenants!***

Oh yeah, they exist! **They're the Pros!** They know how long to stay, how much time you have to evict them, and when to leave! Every month was a struggle to collect rent with excuse after excuse, one after another. The Courthouse became my second job just to file papers to evict! On a monthly basis, we were either serving notice or trying to renovate to get another tenant after the property was wrecked and abandoned! The expenses were high, the bank account dwindled, and the bills kept coming each and every month! Thank God we made sure to separate the business from our personal funds. This went on for several years, and at times it started to affect our marriage. We started to play the blame game and use each other as scapegoats. Thank God we were strong enough to step away and evaluate the situation or I fear it would have destroyed our marriage.

Cause and Effect

We've all heard the saying that for every cause there is an effect! We decided enough is enough, as our houses emptied along with our bank account. We decided to let them go one by one. (The hardest *effect* was watching my credit score plummet to a low 500 from a high 700!) I felt like such a failure as we worked so hard and were left to wonder what went wrong! We promised not to blame each other, but sometimes that was easier said than done!

Now What? Where Do We Go From Here?

The B Word! Have you ever known anyone who filed bankruptcy? Have you ever thought about filing bankruptcy? How did you feel? Who did you tell and what was their reaction? Have you ever felt like you were drowning? Imagine being in a wave pool having lots of fun, but you're not the most skilled swimmer so you take it slow. You're doing pretty well jumping the waves and everything is fine, but then you miss a wave and go under! You try to recover, but every time you try to adjust, you go deeper and further in until you realize that the only way to survive is to just **let go!** You go under, but you start to see your way clear and swim for the stairs, making it out alive! (This actually happened to me and this is the way I felt when we were experiencing our financial woes!) You say to yourself, how did I get here and why is this happening to me? Where do I go from here? I want you to know that you're not in it alone and you can recover!

Webster's Dictionary defines bankruptcy as: 1. *The state of being or becoming bankrupt, 2. Utter ruin, failure, depletion, or the like.*

Wikipedia defines it as "a legally declared inability or impairment of ability of an individual or organization to pay its creditors."

I relate bankruptcy to being a teenager who accidentally gets pregnant and everyone says they won't judge, but instead will support her. But she knows that they're all talking behind her back! What was she thinking? How did she let this happen and what is she going to do now?!

The B Word: That Ugly Word!

The second hardest thing for me to accept was being told that I had to sever all ties with my current financial institution! I had to close my bank account because I had opened loans with them and I felt like a thief in the night! My attorney said, "It's common for people to think that their financial institutes are their friends, but your 'banking friends' have made a lot of you. He explained that large corporations file bankruptcy all the time and call it ***Restructuring!*** I cringed at the mere thought of the words coming out of my mouth! *I'm in **Bankruptcy*** and how and why did this happen to me? I am a good person, take care of my business and take care of others!

Did You Know?

Statistics show that over 150 million people file bankruptcy on a yearly basis! In 2008, personal bankruptcy rates were up almost 30 percent, the highest since the new bankruptcy law took effect in 2005. Young adults/women are carrying almost twice as much student loan debt when they graduate as graduates did a decade ago, says Tamara Draut, co-author of *Generation Broke*. "And they're trying to make their way in a job market that is filled with uncertainty and insecurity."

I recently learned about a term called sexually transmitted debt! It is a flippant term for a serious problem. Sometimes called 'relationship debt,' it relates to the situation where a woman becomes liable for paying her partner or ex-partner's debts. This could be because she's signed a loan contract as a co-borrower or guarantor, has agreed to become a silent director of his company, or has signed a mortgage so he can obtain a loan. The National Credit Code states that every attempt must be made to redeem the money owed by the borrower before pursuing the guarantor. But the reality is that if you have more assets than your partner, earn more money, or are easier to find, you're more likely to be chased for debts owing. As a co-borrower, you may find yourself solely responsible for a debt from which you have received no benefit.

According to a recent survey conducted by the National Association for Business Economics (www.nabe.com) the combined threat of subprime loan defaults and excessive indebtedness has overtaken terrorism and the Middle East as the biggest short-term threat to the U.S. economy. 32% of the survey participants cited loan defaults and excessive debt as the biggest threat, compared to only 20% citing terrorism as the biggest threat. (source: Dan Seymour, Associated Press)

Myths and Facts About Bankruptcy:

Personal bankruptcy is a very undesirable situation. Often caused by sudden changes in your financial situation due to medical emergencies, unemployment, excessive debt or divorce, filing for personal bankruptcy should be considered a responsible step towards regaining financial freedom. If you are considering filing for personal bankruptcy, here are some of the myths and facts about it.

Myth #1: You cannot file for personal bankruptcy.

Contrary to this myth, changes made by the US Congress in 2005 allow any debtor to file for personal bankruptcy. Bankruptcy is also governed by state laws. For instance, if you file bankruptcy in Arizona, Arizona bankruptcy lawyers and Phoenix bankruptcy lawyers can help you determine whether you qualify for a Chapter 7 (liquidation of assets) or Chapter 13 (re-organization) bankruptcy.

Myth#2: Filing for personal bankruptcy is embarrassing.

If you do not file for bankruptcy, it will actually be even more embarrassing to be hounded by your creditors. Taking charge of your financial situation and owing up to your responsibilities is actually admirable and should be something to be proud of.

Myth#3: You will always have a bad credit score.

If you must know, the completion of personal bankruptcy proceedings will clear all previous credit records allowing you to begin with a new and clean slate.

Myth#4: You can only file for personal bankruptcy once in your lifetime.

If you filed for a Chapter 7 bankruptcy, you will need to wait a period of eight years before you can file for the next Chapter 7 bankruptcy. On the other hand, you can file for a Chapter 13 bankruptcy as often as your situation requires.

Myth#5: Personal bankruptcy means losing everything you have.

On the contrary, bankruptcy is designed to protect a debtor from losing all assets and at the same time find a way for all the debt to be settled.

Myth#6: Filing for personal bankruptcy is hard to do.

Anyone can file a personal bankruptcy. You will have no difficulties at all. If you want, you can use bankruptcy lawyers to help you every step of the way.

Personal bankruptcy is a serious but effective solution to your financial problems. Before you file for one, make sure that you have explored all available bankruptcy alternatives.

There is always someone else who's worst off than you! But don't find yourself saying that this situation is not your fault. Don't discount the bankruptcy by making someone else's crisis greater than your own.

Take responsibility for your bankruptcy!

Webster Dictionary defines Responsibility as:

1. The state or fact of being responsible.

2. An instance of being responsible: *The responsibility for this mess is yours!*

3. A particular burden of obligation upon one who is responsible: *the responsibilities of authority.*

4. A person or thing for which one is responsible: *A child is a responsibility to its parents.*

5. Reliability or dependability, esp. in meeting debts or payments.

I define it as a time in your life where you decided enough is enough and you can't go any further until you take care of what's in front of you now!

Some Reasons for Filing Bankruptcy:

1. Fraud/Identity theft

2. Student loans

3. Too much credit

4. Loss of income/employment

5. Business didn't make it

6. Divorce

7. Heaven forbid, death

8. Living beyond your means

9. Medical bills

The list goes on and on and some reasons haven't even been invented yet!

Some Ways to Avoid This If at All Possible:

1. Become more conscious of your spending.

2. Don't loan more than you can afford to give.

3. Avoid using credit cards as much as possible – set a limit. If you can't afford to pay it off in a month, you don't use it.

4. Just remember, your credit score is your "life til death do you part!" You are married to it and go through your ups and downs, but know it is with you all the time, for good or bad.

Well, you asked yourself, why did this happen to me? Bad things happen to good people all of the time! You just have to push through it and tell yourself you can do it, get through it and with God all things are possible. Know that this is a test and you will pass with flying colors.

As for me, our journey has just begun! Check back with me in about five years and I'll let you know how it turned out.

ABOUT THE AUTHOR

DIANNA L CURRINGTON-HEARD

Dianna L. Currington-Heard, a Performance Improvement, Learning and Development Facilitator with extensive Human Resources Management, Coaching and Leadership experience. Dianna is the President and Chief Executive Officer of two separate and distinctly exceptional businesses: "Girls to Pearls, Inc." (non-profit) and "Global Transformations, Inc.," (profit).

"Girls to Pearls, Inc." through a series of formal and informal interactive workshops and outreach activities are designed to meet the needs of Girls, local Municipalities, Churches, and other Community Groups interested in the positive development of Girls, ages 9 to 19 years. The vision of GTP is to inspire and influence their intellectual and spiritual growth, health and well-being, social etiquette, and community service as they transition to womanhood. Workshops consist of:

- Promoting Positive Self-Esteem As They (Girls) Form An Appreciation For Their Individuality;
- Establishing And Maintaining Nurturing Relationships;
- Developing Self-Discipline and Social Confidence;
- Making Wise Decisions;
- Setting Goals To Optimize Positive Results; and
- Developing A Sense Of Duty Through Community Awareness

On May 24th, 2010, Apostle John L. Mohorn, Jr., Pastor of The Word Of The Living God Ministries located in Pompano Beach, FL introduced "Girls to Pearls" as an outreach program for the congregation's Youth.

"Global Transformations, Inc." A Team of experts skilled in the strategic development of Concepts, People, and Growing Organizations can facilitate and lead an organization through change and transformation by examining goals and objectives to meet customers present needs; current processes and employee efficiency; assist with implementation of action plans; and perform periodic assessments for continuous improvement to maximize business results.

Area of Expertise: Human Resource Management and Employee Relations, Facilitating and Leading Change to Improve Business Results and Employee Efficiency; Personal Coaching; Teen Counseling; Paralegal-Judge Advocate General's Corps(U.S. Navy), Military Justice.

Education/Training:
Bachelors of Science. Excelsior/Regents College; Florida Atlantic University; University of Maryland; University of San Diego; U.S. Naval Justice School.; Certification in Organizational Development; Certified Lawyer's Assistant; Society of Human Resource Management (SHRM) Certification. Excelsior/Regents College; Florida Atlantic University; University of Maryland; Broward College; University of San Diego; U.S. Naval Justice School. Bachelors of Science; Certificate in Organizational Development; Certified Lawyer's Assistant; Society of Human Resource Management (SHRM) Certification.

Course of Study: Sociology; Business Administration and Human Resources Management; Organizational Development and Strategic Planning; Criminal justice and Family Law; Teen Self-Esteem and Social Etiquette.

Associations: U.S. Naval Fleet Reserve Association, Branch 256, Pompano Beach, FL; South Florida Chapter of Certified Public Managers (CPM); International Society for Performance Improvement (ISPI); South Florida Organizational Development Network (SFLODN); National Association of Professional Women (NAPW).

Hobbies: Reading, Performing Arts, Singing•
Dianna is a 20 year veteran of U.S. Naval Service and a Fort Lauderdale native. She is the daughter of Johnny A. Currington (deceased) and Myrtle Porter-Currington; Sister of Jon A. Currington and Rosalind D. Currington. Dianna is the mother of two Sons: Victor L. Coleman II and Anthony A. Heard.

TWENTY-ONE

THE ART OF FORGIVENESS

By Dianna Currington Heard

When I considered accepting the offer of writing this chapter, I believed I had something to offer others who may have found themselves in a place of isolation when a life experience so traumatic, so uninvited, so not welcomed is imposed upon you as a result of another's actions, or a decision you made causes such pain that it shakes you to your very core.

However, as I started to put pen to paper trying to take myself back through the emotions and struggle to survive a moment in time, my traumatic period, it became apparent to me that 'My' experience, 'My' pain was not unique. Truth be told, it was 'My Turn.' The difference I found was how 'I' managed the pain. How did I pick up the pieces of a shattered life? I was determined to survive. By taking on forgiveness as an art, as I put into practice the act of forgiveness, I was able to reach self-preservation. Considering the consequence of unforgiveness versus the benefits of granting forgiveness, I gained the reward of self-empowerment.

My story begins and will end with God. I had already started my walk with God prior to the breakup of my marriage to a man I believed I would love forever. When the breakup occurred as a result of a fifteen year adulterous affair, (told you it was not unique), and the subsequent birth of their beautiful daughter, I was forced to "deal" with life.

To say I was devastated would be an understatement. I loved being married; I loved being married to my husband. There were the expected emotional stages of denial, pleading, depression, many, many, many tears, guilt, and loss of self-esteem. Missing from these emotions were anger and bitterness. I remember a great sadness for my husband and for myself. A deep sadness because he gave up, he gave up on me and on us.

Searching for the answer to the proverbial "Why?" was a constant quest, playing back every detail of the marriage at the point of the start up of their affair. I continued to relive every episode of the breakup with anyone polite enough to listen. During one very hysterical outburst, it became apparent I was in serious emotional trouble. I likened it to having an outer body experience, to realize there really is a thin line between sanity and insanity. God bought to my remembrance His word, "..........*count it all joy when you fall into various trials; ....knowing that the testing of your faith produces patience.*"

In that moment, I made a conscious decision to trust God. I agreed to willingly take this journey with God directing my path. At the onset, through prayer and a prayer partner, I sought to discover my role and take responsibility for my part of the breakup of my marriage. Having been Wife and Mother for twenty-three years, I was alone. As most of my family and friends urged me to 'Get a life,' I set out to redefine my life's direction through God and His divine purpose for my life.

It became clear that before I could move forward, it was necessary for me to forgive my husband, the love of my life, the one God charged with protecting me and our home from the World. More surprising to me was realizing I also found myself having to forgive God. Part of the "Why" had been directed towards God, for surely, as his just daughter, why would He allow this in my life? I knew forgiveness was necessary as evidence of my total trust in God's will for my life and to allow me to attract the kind of love that God has for me.

I soon realized people will come and go in our lives; not everyone can go where you are going. Bad times and awful things are going to happen in your life; and people close to you will be the cause of your pain. Nevertheless, locking away your heart, turning off your emotions to keep people from getting close to you, to prevent future pain is not an excuse for not feeling or failing. As these bad times and awful life experiences happen, and yes, sometimes at the hand of those closest to you, remember,

"Tough times don't last always. Tough people last through it all! What is obtained by love is retained for all times. Hatred proves a burden in reality, for it increases hatred." —Gandhi

There is a Certain "Art" as Well as the "Act" of Forgiveness

Richard Hoefler's book *Will Daylight Come?* includes a homey **illustration** of how sin enslaves and **forgiveness** frees ... It must be dealt with responsibly, honestly, in a decisive **act** of ...

I made a mental list of everything I believed was wrong with my husband and his inability to stay committed to me and our marriage before the concept of forgiveness fell heavily upon me. As evidence of my faith walk in forgiveness, I selectively chose a few of his faults and forgave them, but I hung onto the bigger faults that caused me the most pain. It was not long before I realized that my 'symbolic' act of forgiveness revealed the limits on healing and continued emotional difficulties that persisted in my life. Once I made a conscious decision to forgive everything, the unforeseen effects proved the turning point in my life to allow me to move forward.

"I think you can forgive a little, you can forgive all the way or you cannot forgive at all."—Lynn McGuinn

When Forgiveness Is a Matter of Self-Preservation

The truth of the matter was, I was left to figure this out for myself. After repeatedly asking my husband to share what he believed I contributed to the breakdown of our marriage, he would not clearly state what was missing or how the marriage (I) was not meeting his needs. I endeavored to do the hard work for myself; after all, I aim to be married and do not want a repeat of this episode.

Through self-reflection and accountability, I condemned my God given character traits purposed for the one thing God has commissioned me to do here on Earth. For months, I attempted to change me in order **TO** protect me from future rejection. Unfortunately, this change caused greater disappointment and lower self-esteem. Our Father is gracious, and he sent angels in the form of family, friends, and colleagues who recognized and commented on the changes as 'unauthentic'. It was clear that I had been living an 'unauthentic' life with my husband for the greater part of our marriage. Once the truth about his infidelity was in the open, his interruption of my trust reignited the me I was meant to be. I prayed for forgiveness as God began to grant me the wisdom of knowing that I am uniquely made, designed with the character traits necessary to accomplish my purposed life. As I forgave myself, I was ready to move forward toward a healthy future.

Emotional Well Being Through Forgiveness and the Effect of Memories

As life began again, I became keenly aware I was harboring ill will and I had no tolerance for those who complained or spoke adversely about their spouse or significant other. Such complains or adverse comments conjured up painful memories of past criticisms about me being bossy and controlling.

It was disturbing to discover the effect the role of such painful memories still played on my emotional well being. Painful memories which are usually passed down through observation and conversation, memories capable of perpetuating emotional and psychic pain.

"If we let go of the pain in the memory we can have the memory, but it doesn't control us."—Alexandra Asseily

In my quest to regain emotional well being, I discovered Dr. Kathleen Lawler-Row. Dr. Lawler-Row is a professor of psychology who has conducted extensive research into the effects of forgiveness on the human body. Since 1998, Dr. Lawler-Row has been researching forgiveness and health, examining forgiveness as a general personality style and as a response to a particular betrayal event. She interviews individuals and examines the relationship of forgiveness to blood pressure and heart rate, measured while they recall a hurtful offense.

She also studies how forgiveness is linked to stress, physical health, and successful aging. Having administered over 300 interviews, Lawler-

Row has seen clearly how degrees of forgiveness map onto the body, with resentment and thoughts of revenge associated with higher blood pressure, higher heart rates, and greater levels of stress, depression, and symptoms of physical illness.

Dr. Lawler-Row is the author and co-author of scores of publications and articles and has presented at countless conferences, both nationally and internationally. She is a fellow of the American Psychology Society. Dr. Lawler-Row is Professor and Chair of the Department of Psychology at East Carolina University. Her work provided a renewed commitment for keeping my memories, but allowed forgiveness to erase the pain of those memories, for they (memories) are evidence of my life's experience.

Consequence of Unforgiveness

Unforgiveness is something that can hold us back from escaping the corruption of sin and living for God. Unforgiveness comes in many forms, such as bitterness, hatred, malice, holding grudges and resentment. It can actually block God's forgiveness of our sin and provides a foothold for the satan to influence our lives.

During my ordeal, oddly enough, I was more concerned with the effect and damage unforgiveness would leave upon my heart. My concern was for my future Boaz. I declared, "I will be able to love again with my whole heart! No way will I risk carrying bitterness, hatred, malice or resentment in my heart to be showered on someone undeserving."

"We tend to talk about justice far more often in every community that's been in turmoil and we rarely talk about forgiveness and mercy."
—Robert Enright

Benefits From Your Forgiveness

Being a child of God, I have been taught that if you forgive those who trespass against you, our heavenly Father will also forgive us (me). But if I did not forgive those who commit trespasses, neither will my Father forgive my sins.

What more could I ask? It was then a matter of how do I gain victory by doing what is right while it still felt so wrong, wrong to forgive? Forgive the one who had caused such indescribable pain, which totally consumed every area of your life. I started the "Act" of forgiveness in bits and pieces! I did not bite off more than I could swallow. It was a lifestyle change toward forgiveness with God leading the way.

I practiced rituals, a series of focused actions, with forgiveness as my goal. Focused on letting go in order to forgive, I used controlled thoughts as a tool to break through tightly held patterns, which I recognized as self-sabotaging and self-destructive behavior.

"If we learn to open our hearts, then anyone, including the people who drive us crazy, can be our teacher."—Pema Chodron

Self-Empowerment In The Act Of Forgiveness

Through my journey to 'manage' my pain, my determination to pick up the pieces, to survive by taking on forgiveness as an art in the act of forgiveness with God's guidance, I was able to achieve self-preservation. Having considered the consequence of unforgiveness versus the benefits of granting forgiveness earned me the reward of self-empowerment. Forgiveness is an ongoing process rather than a one-time **act.**

The Art and Act of Forgiveness

Knowledge is Power! I found faith, honesty, integrity and responsibility are the cornerstones for staying the course in my demonstration of forgiveness as a process. Moreover, I believe it is possible for flawed and ordinary people to forgive others and themselves. If you are ready to commit to forgiveness, a few of my rituals, focused actions for letting go in order to forgive, are listed. I pray you find inner peace, realize you are uniquely made, and designed with the character traits necessary to accomplish your God purposed life.

Taking Off the Mask:

- Identify the hurt: *You inflicted upon someone; someone inflicted on you; you inflicted upon yourself*

- Describe your emotional feelings: *I trusted someone and got hurt; I should have known better; I want to feel safe again; I want justice; I keep replaying the event; I find it hard to trust anyone.*

- Put your hurt into words: *I want to be understood and loved 'as I am,' strong, confident, aggressive, tender, nurturing and giving, flaws and all."*

Plan your Act of Forgiveness:

- Write down actions to intentionally add love and forgiveness to your life. You can practice on a daily basis, such as demonstrate simple affection or self-forgiveness.

- Share actions with those who cause trespass, friend or family member and/or support each other in becoming more loving and forgiving.

- Check your behavior: As you start practicing these actions into your life, practice hearing yourself talk. After each verbal encounter, ask yourself, *Did I say something kind?* and *Did I say something unkind?* Apologize for any unkind statements. Notice what happens. *Note how it makes you feel and whether you detect any shifts in your relationships.*

Journaling:

Writing regularly in a journal to encourage you to see life experiences and emotions more clearly, to better understand your own behavior, and explore your attitudes.

- Write or draw the events of the day or a single event to convey your feelings. If the day was an unpleasant experience, remember to look for a positive "take away" lesson learned from having lived through the experience. Do not forget the 'AHAA!' moments, those moments that take your breath away.

- Make a list of people, animals, things, and qualities in yourself and others that you love most. Ask family and friends to share things they love with you.

- Describe a moment when you felt truly loved. What was it about that experience that made you feel loved?

- Describe something you witnessed that showed you are executing your decision to forgive.

- Look for opportunities to express kindness to someone in words or actions. At the end of the day, record in your journal the acts of service you did.

- Write a statement of affirmation to renew your commitment to forgive.

Your Daily Focus: Concentrate each day on Faith, Life, Health, and Strength.

Celebrate You! At the same time you are practicing the art of forgiveness, do not forget to remind yourself about your own fine qualities. Do not wait to be invited for a night out on the town or to go to dinner or the movies with the girls; take yourself. Rediscover those areas of interest you previously put away; sign up for a college course, travel, start a business, volunteer at your church or in the community. Up for a makeover? – Go for it!

You Are Nearing the End of Your Journey

Forgiveness does not necessarily occur after the wrong has been made right. Indeed, 'the right' in the eye of the beholder may never come, or perhaps not in the form envisioned. As our Creator, God knows us well, even before we were born, even while we were still in our mother's womb, He loves and has plans for us. Rest assured with unwavering certainty, forgiveness and fairness will manifest according to the will of God.

Notes:

ABOUT THE AUTHOR

SAMONE DARDEN-LETT

Samone Darden-Lett, an inspirational speaker and author has a desire to see people set free; to see men and women free of the shackles and chains that the burdens of life dished out. Her purpose is helping people realize two things: how to walk in their divine purpose and destiny and how to know their true identity and worth. Samone has found that identity and worth aren't found in a man or a woman but in the Heavenly Father. "It is in Him we can find our wholeness". Born and raised in Brooklyn, New York, Samone Darden-Lett has walked a life of personal discovery, hard lessons, and spiritual growth. "My mission is to share with others how to be set free from the adversities of life; God has plans for each of us whether we believe it or not." Samone served her country in the United States Army, where she lent her skills as a Food Specialist while stationed in Germany. She holds an Associates Degree in Hospitality Management and has also graduated Cum Laude from Le Cordon Bleu in Culinary Arts & Management. Samone is active monthly in the spiritual restoration of young women in the State of Florida. At The Lowell Correctional Facility in Ocala Florida, Samone was part of prison ministry. Through her local church she also mentored women at the Orlando Women's Work Release Department, assisting them in re-entry to daily life after incarceration. She is an entrepreneur, author, mentor, wife, and is dedicated daily to the plans God has for her future. Currently residing in Orlando, Florida, she owns Wishful Concepts, a catering business and is also working on other entrepreneurial ventures such as skincare, hair care, and health enhancement products. Presently, she is pursuing her Bachelors and Masters Degrees in Christian Counseling.

Contact:
Samone-Darden Lett
PO Box 140731
Orlando, FL 32814
Telephone: 866.925.7776
Web: http://www.samonedarden.com
Email: befree@samonedarden.com

TWENTY-TWO

ABANDONMENT

By Samone Darden

I woke up one morning and sent my pastor's wife an email wanting to know if it would be okay in God's eyes to divorce my husband and not solely make a decision based upon my emotions. My church already knew my situation, my story and my experiences with my ex-husband. I was faced with a dilemma and one question bombarded my mind. "What should I do?" Her response was simply, "Samone, you have been abandoned. Your husband left you without warning."

a·ban·don—*1. to leave completely and finally; forsake utterly; desert: to abandon one's farm; to abandon a child; to abandon a sinking ship. 2. to give up; discontinue; withdraw from: to abandon a research project; to abandon hopes for a stage career. 3. to give up the control of: to abandon a city to an enemy army. 4. to yield (oneself) without restraint or moderation; give (oneself) over to natural impulses, usually without self-control: to abandon oneself to grief. 5. Law. to cast away, leave, or desert, as property or a child.* (Dictionary.com)

"So be strong and courageous! Do not be afraid and do not panic before them. For the LORD your God will personally go ahead of you. He will neither fail you nor abandon you."
—Deuteronomy 31:6, New Living Translation

"Even if my father and mother abandon me, the LORD will hold me close."
—Psalm 27:10, New Living Translation

Although many words were said to me in the conversation with my pastor's wife, that word *abandoned* was burned into my heart for a long time. It was not until that conversation with my pastor's wife did truth come to me about what had happened to me. Not only did he commit adultery, but he left me without warning or explanation. He simply left without an email, voice message, or letter. Once again the feeling of abandonment set in because of the selfish actions of someone I sincerely loved and believed loved me in return. I remember the coldness of my spirit, the feelings of numbness and anger; then the tears fell once anger and numbness expired. In the midst of my emotions, God still spoke to me about restoration, but God's words conflicted with the painful reality. For my relationship to be restored, it would require the willing participation of both partners.

But based on my ex-husband's actions and obvious choices, it would seem restoration wasn't going to happen; at least not with our marriage and not in the ways interpreted by God. Soon after, divorce papers were filed and freedom was granted to escape this emotionally traumatic union. But even though papers were filed presenting my freedom from this situation, much of my pain remained dormant and active in my heart preventing me from loving freely. The feelings of betrayal and abandonment were swept under the rug, along with many other issues, for years. I've learned that sweeping issues under the rug prevents true growth and blocks spiritual freedom. Like so many of us, never would I have guessed that what I had been suffering from for many years was entitled, "Abandonment."

Understanding Abandonment Patterns and Origins

To break any pattern in our lives, we must face ourselves on a deeper level, even levels that involve looking back into the infancy stages of our lives. While on your journey to heal, there must be an acknowledgment about emotional issues originating from sources of much deeper pain. Abandonment mainly stems from childhood and in my childhood not knowing my father created the catalyst for feeling abandoned. My memories of my father were based on conversations with him over the phone, sharing promises that were never fulfilled; empty promises of birthday plans and deliveries of gifts that just never manifested. When the time presented itself to meet him, it resulted in disaster from not knowing his function as a father or my role as a daughter. Greeting him became challenging. Was I supposed to call him "Dad" or "John"? I wasn't sure how to interact with this man who was supposed to be my father.

Later on in my childhood, the disappearance of my step father, who relocated to California without any notice or warning, also pierced my heart; another notch in the belt of feeling abandoned by others. Or for instance, my mother verbalized every moment humorously that she wanted a boy. Even in humor her words were disturbing. At times my mother gave me the impression that she really didn't want me, or wished I had been a boy. During my childhood my grandmother planted her love in my heart. My grandmother was my greatest love and seeing her leave this Earth was one of the toughest things I've experienced. Even experiencing the death of a family member or friend can stir up emotions of abandonment. Staring at her casket during her funeral crushed me emotionally and only intensified my feelings of abandonment. Throughout my childhood, abandonment continued to distort my perspective on relationships, love, and connections with others. My relationship with God, however, brought me to a road of healing. Healing from those who didn't see value in our connection, left my life through natural causes, or just never expressed their love to me in a manner in which I could have understood.

Facing Child Abandonment Issues

Many of us during childhood were verbally or physically abused and worse. Some had to live with the reality of having absentee parents. A resource that was informative in learning more about childhood abandonment issues was a behavioral science textbook supplied to students at Full Sail University. It concluded that the infant stages of humans present the initial opportunity to build trust with others. "Infants are delivered into the world with fundamental physiological needs. Their caregivers must be willing and able to satisfy these requirements. Trust at its most basic level arises when an infant can sense that its parents can be depended upon for fulfillment of its needs. If trust is developed successfully, the child acquires confidence and security in the world, and retains this underlying sense of stability, even when posed with a threat."

Due to my lack of positive experiences, these facts present truth to my struggles. What my situations have taught is that trusting or mistrusting others is learned through social conditions and parenting.

Parents who choose to relinquish their duties set their children up for spiritual failure. I truly believe that my childhood experiences were unhealthy. If I had been given the opportunity to learn how to trust, my childhood would've been embraced fully. Learning to embrace trust would have strengthened my foundation as a child, enhanced my self-esteem, and taught me how to establish stronger connections and communication with others. "The failure to complete this stage successfully can diminish the infant's future propensity for developing trust and can result in heightened fears, anxieties and insecurities."

One day in prayer the Lord showed me a little girl sitting on the edge of a bed swinging her feet; it was me at a younger age. This younger version of me had been maintaining control over my growth by harboring the events from my past and blocking true love from entering in. She had been inside of me for years living in pain; afraid that things would always be the same. This was my vision granted by God through prayer, but for many, their inner child still lives inside of them, being the gatekeeper of their heart and soul. There must come a time when you face that hurt inner child, confront it and let it know that this time you're going to be okay and healing will break forth. *"Then your light shall break forth like the morning, your healing shall spring forth speedily, and your righteousness shall go before you; The glory of the LORD shall be your rear guard."*—Isaiah 58:8, New King James Version

To start on your journey of seeking out your inner child, here are some thoughts to consider:

1. Children who have been abandoned may have had difficulty expressing their emotions freely. How should the communication have been established with your family members growing up?

2. Understanding how feelings should be expressed is a lesson that is often not taught at home. How should self-expression have been encouraged growing up? Should it have been encouraged or banned?

3. Daily words of affirmation help to encourage children daily. What positive words or statements should have been told to you that could have increased your self-esteem?

4. When confidentiality is maintained between a parent and a child, the level of trust is strong. Were there any situations where a parent or guardian broke confidentiality and it then became hard for you to trust?

Abandonment and Personalities

Abandonment often times creates two types of personality traits: passive and passive aggressive. The passive personality trait tends to seek out love regardless of the negative outcomes of their pursuits. Promiscuity toward the opposite sex is often the habitual nature of the passive individual. This type can suffer from burdening shame and guilt. Enduring verbal and physical abuse and accepting manipulation from others highlights some of the characteristics of the passive personality dealing with abandonment. The passive-aggressive personality living with abandonment issues walks through life with very hard exteriors. This is something that I identify with. They become defensive quickly when correction comes their way regarding errors and personal mistakes. They find it very challenging to express emotions of love, affection and concern. A life of isolation fits this personality type best and severing communication with friends and loved ones becomes an easy process.

A passive-aggressive can find comfort in living in isolation and straying from interpersonal responsibilities. Dependency, competition (*desire to prove oneself*), and intimacy are some other areas that passive-aggressive individuals struggle with. No matter the personality types struggling with abandonment, many are going about it in the wrong way. How can help arrive to so many if hearts are hardened and love is hard to receive? Some of us are so hardheaded that it may require a Saul/Paul biblical experience, bringing humility to us by God himself. (Acts 9:1-22)

What Else is Affected?

With intimacy, one has to bear all to truly experience it with someone. The desire to love passionately is in each and every one of us. Due to certain abandonment issues however, the closer the connection becomes, the more we often times find ourselves holding back or withdrawing. Lack of trust keeps us from sharing and exposing everything about ourselves, which can hinder us from walking in real love. We want full control at all times. But if we think about it, what do we really have control over? Has the little control we do have helped or hindered us? To be honest, it hasn't helped me much. After analyzing my relationships from the past, there have always been barriers that were kept up between me and the person trying to establish a relationship with me; for years I could never allow myself to be free in relationships. Hesitation often set in within so many situations, from expressing myself verbally, to initiating physical contact i.e., a pat on the back, a hug, holding someone's hand or even a high five for doing a good job. There was no comfort in my own sensuality of being a woman. I lacked the knowledge of how to embrace that part of me, so for years I continued down the same path of pretending to have all the answers.

It's time we shake our fists in the face of the enemy and tell abandonment to no longer keep us down. The enemy's goal is to continue to keep us down, and to draw strength from our pain in every moment of every day. The truth of the matter is that the enemy is afraid of our power to love and form connections with others. With love we can conquer anything. Love can cast out all fear. It allows us to be free of torment, no longer living like a caged bird afraid to sing. *"Love has been perfected among us in this: that we may have boldness in the day of judgment; because as He is, so are we in this world. There is no fear in love; but perfect love casts out fear, because fear involves torment. But he who fears has not been made perfect in love."* 1 John 4:17-18, New King James Version

I want to urge all to not only make tempers, past frustrations, anger, guilt, and all other excuses to take a back seat, but kick them out of the car! Dare to believe you can receive your healing as I am learning to receive mine. Stand in the fire and allow the things of the past to be burned away, even if it hurts! Tears and outbursts are all part of the process of standing in the fire, but do not run away; tough it out and know that you are not standing alone. As the Lord burns and pulls away the heavy burdens, He will refill you with not only more love, but He will provide you with the eagerness to pursue it. Don't run away from the opportunity to receive your healing. Do whatever is needed, no matter how ugly the feelings experienced during the process; tough it out. Now personally, crying was not an option for me, and never was it shown in front of people. I felt it showed a sign of weakness, but my growth has taught me its strength and purpose. The shedding of tears is part of releasing burdens.

Being blessed with an opportunity to contribute to this book has allowed me to do further research into abandonment and the subject matter revolving around it. Never did I truly realize that many of my struggles with trust, love, and emotional expression originated from this topic of abandonment. This self-discovery provided me with an epiphany about the truth of my abandonment issues. To receive all the things God had for my life, making peace with my past, forgiving people, and letting go were all requirements. Even though a strong man has now entered my life as my husband through the promises of God, I needed to be prepared for my mate by working on myself first. To survive, everyone needs a defense mechanism. It is through these protective mechanisms that we survive difficult and challenging situations. But there comes a time in our lives when letting go and tearing down walls is needed if we are to achieve emotional freedom. If we don't let down our guard, we won't be able to enjoy new opportunities or see the possibilities that lie ahead. It says in the Word to give no place to the devil. *"Leave no [such] room or foothold for the devil [give no opportunity to him].* —Ephesians 4:27, Amplified Bible. The same way that we give no room to the devil, we also present no opportunity for those who have come to nurture, restore, uplift, and change our lives.

Why is it so hard for us to understand true love? The Bible states that love is from God. In fact, the Bible says, "God is love." Love is one of the primary characteristics of God. It's the greatest command in the Bible. It also says its unconditional. (Matthew 22:36-40). To put it simply, we want to experience sacrificial love; a love that is based on **self-sacrifice** with the pure motivation being to alleviate the suffering of others. Sacrificial love isn't about counting the faults and mistakes of others. Sacrificial love is agape love. An example of sacrificial love is in John 13:1-11 where Jesus washes the disciple's feet. Another example can be found when Jesus died on the cross for our sins. Paul, one of Jesus' disciples, was sentenced to prison and tormented, all for the love of the church. Every one of us will have an "experience moment" with God. Within these types of moments lay an opportunity to change our perspective on life forever. Saul, (*whose name got changed to Paul, Acts 9:1-22*) had an experience with Jesus so strong it knocked him to the ground and he was struck blind for three days. He knew the only Force on this planet with that much power to stop him dead in his tracks was the Lord. When he got knocked down, he heard the voice of the Lord speak. He cried out, *"Who are you, lord?"* Then, *"What should I do, Lord?"*—Acts 22:7-14.

Abandonment Issues Concerning The Church

When hearts become hurt and emotional burdens become heavy, there are those that seek guidance through many means; some seek out religious institutions. For Christians, the church has been a refuge for the sick, poor, and the spiritually burdened. Pastors, ministers, clergy, priests, and congregation members have abandoned their duties to God without the acknowledgement of their personal behavior. The church has been operating solely out of tradition and laws. The church has forgotten the key element in Christianity which is an intimate, honest, and pure relationship with God. Laws of the church often prevent leaders from maintaining a sincere and compassionate relationship with the body of Christ. Church leaders have forgotten their own paths and experiences with God, often passing judgment on those who are lost. They're transforming into cold, arrogant, and insensitive individuals towards God's sheep. As a result, the lost are returning back to a life of pain, confusion and despair. For many lost sheep, the church was their last hope to gain encouragement and freedom from a life of emotional burden. Do many often find it? Unfortunately, the answer is no. Many are walking away bruised and spiritually unaided which propels them into a life of disbelief, prostitution, addiction, prison, and in many cases death, either by crime or suicide. Abandonment is happening in the church. When the very thing that so many people turn to fails, we are all doomed to have faith in nothing. That includes love, relationships, successful opportunities, and spiritual deliverance. So many have lost hope in parents, teachers, politicians, government, and unfortunately the Lord's representatives. How do we get the spiritually abandoned back on the pathway of healing? First, there needs to be a quick education about developing a relationship with God. Relationship means direct and honest communication with our Creator. Pastors, ministers, priests and other church leaders are not re-incarnations of God; they are humans with the responsibility to lead others to Christ. There must be consistent study of the Word and prayer. God speaks to us and if we are willing to make time to develop a relationship with God, He will lead us toward healing.

Journey Towards Your Healing

1. Embrace the journey to heal by addressing key issues that have affected you; observe your upbringing and past relationships.

2. Prepare to walk on a spiritual journey with our Creator. Don't turn back while soul searching. Inner dialogue will help, and if necessary, daily journal writing. Be willing to venture into any dark, painful, or emotionally uncomfortable place that may challenge your healing.

3. Seek support through counseling, mentorship programs, or family support groups.

4. Focus daily on rebuilding a new mindset through consistent daily affirmations and prayers; begin to embrace your value and reject the negative things.

5. As you walk on this daily journey, your mind, spirit, and heart will begin to align, causing change to occur. Embrace it, regardless of the difficulties that may arise.

6. Even though change for the better will be happening, there will be moments of tears, yelling, and recollecting the past and its hardships; this is normal and it too shall pass.

7. Most importantly, surround yourself with others who reinforce your journey towards healing, for instance supportive friends that provide encouragement daily, those that speak life and not death. *"The tongue has the power of life and death, and those who love it will eat its fruit."*—Proverbs 18:21, New International Version

Personal Journey Activity

We've established that abandonment can rear its ugly head in many forms. Picture a tree with its many roots—roots taking form in anger, low-self esteem, pride, alcoholism, drugs, gluttony, insecurity, lack of trust and depression. In order to kill the tree the roots must be pulled out. So the question is, do abandonment issues ever go away? Yes, once you face them, but as long as you run, your issues will never go away. Here are some important things to consider:

What are you MOST afraid of?

• Giving love and receiving love.

- Getting hurt again or being left.

- Not trusting.

- Once the truth is revealed, will the person dear to us leave?

- Will I live in isolation forever?

- I won't overcome the pain.

- No one really cares for me.

- Will I be protected by others who love me?

- The pain is just too much to deal with.

- I might expose too many emotions.

- Depending on others for help

- Needing approval of others

- I can't do anything right, like I will mess up again.

- I am afraid of knowing the truths inside of my heart.

- I am anxious and afraid.

May you be blessed on your journey to face your abandonment issues and know that God is with you EVERY step of the way. You are not alone.

ABOUT THE AUTHOR

MICHAEL COLEMAN

Michael Coleman holds a Master of Business Administration from the University of Indianapolis, and Bachelor of Science Degree in Political Science from Western Illinois University. Mike has been involved in retail management, training, and human resources for more than 25 years.

Mike Coleman is President and Founder of the Mike Coleman Institute, a resource organization dedicated to improving the professional, personal, and family life of men. Michael is a member of the National Fatherhood Initiative (NFI). The mission of NFI is *"To improve the well-being of children by increasing the proportion of children growing up with involved, responsible, and committed fathers."*

In 2002, Mike attended a seminar offered by the Professional Woman Network (PWN). The information presented was so powerful he decided to join PWN. Mike has used the unique perspectives and insights gained from PWN to better understand the dynamics between men and women.

Mr. Coleman is a PWN certified trainer in professional presentation skills, women's wellness, and diversity issues. Mr. Coleman has offered programs on family wellness, teen development, and workplace diversity. Inspired by the work of PWN and NFI, Michael is developing **retaildad.com** a resource network for men in the retail industry.

Currently living in Dallas, Texas with his family, Mike is a devoted husband, and father of 2 boys. He is an active member of Grace Outreach Church in Plano, TX.

"This chapter is dedicated to my PWN sisters for helping me to realize the difference between a man and a jerk.

Contact:
Retaildad
Box 851
Frisco, TX 75034
mikec@reaildad.com
www.reaildad.com
www.protrain.net

TWENTY-THREE

YOU CAN'T FIX A BAD BOY!

By Mike Coleman

Frank describes a common relationship scenario: "When Lisa and I started seeing each other, it was magic! We were like soul-mates. I would start to say something, and she would complete my sentence. I could do no wrong. She seemed to understand and satisfy my every need. After about three months, something happened; she suddenly changed. Lisa told me that I needed to stop smoking cigarettes. I was okay with that, in fact I thought it was cute she was looking out for my well-being. Next, Lisa didn't approve of the amount of time I was spending with the guys. But it got worse; she started nagging me about spending too much time and money on poker night, and not enough time with her. I couldn't talk to my ex-girlfriend. The last straw was when she threw away my copies of Playboy magazine. What happened to that sweet little girl that would hold on to every word I spoke? What happened to the shy girl that would blush when I looked at her from across a crowded room? That girl vanished inside the body of a monster. In three short months, I went from hero to zero. I was lost; no clue about what I did or what she wanted in our relationship."

Men and Women Want Different Things in a Relationship.

Men are from Mars, and women are from Venus. Each gender has uniquely different needs that must be satisfied in a relationship for true happiness to exist. Men are frustrated in relationships because they don't understand what women want. In the case of Frank and Lisa, Frank had no clue why Lisa wanted to change the terms of the relationship. Frank felt that if Lisa was with him, she must have accepted him. When a man pursues a woman, he is primarily focused on finding the mate that will meet his needs (her needs are secondary, at best).

Women want safety and security in a relationship. Her decision to get into a relationship is serious business; she is looking for a sense of permanence. Regardless of her socioeconomic status, she needs to feel that she is on solid ground. Casual dating is so very frustrating, because it lacks emotional stability. She spends a lot of time trying to improve the relationship to meet her unique expectations. It is important that her boyfriend is equally committed to the same goal. If he is truly invested, changing his ways to improve the partnership should be easy.

Problems occur when the guy is not willing to change his personality to match her desires. To the dismay of millions of women, they can't always expect a man to change. Often times she interprets his resistance to change as a lack of interest or selfishness. Guys become irritated by excessive demands to become someone different. It is like buying a Ford truck, and then being upset that it does not perform like a Mercedes Benz. A woman simply can't decide to date a guy, become more serious with him, and then expect him to do a personality makeover.

Is He a Gentleman or a Jerk?

If we accept that women have a natural tendency for changing a relationship, then the real issue becomes, is he worth the effort? Single, divorced, and widowed women all have the same question; when I meet this guy, how do I know if he is a winner or a loser? The ideal man comes in many sizes, shapes, and colors. Prince Charming might not have expensive cars, summer houses, or an 850 FICO score. Character and personality is what separates a gentleman from a jerk.

- A gentleman is kind, attentive, resourceful, and responsible.

- A gentleman does not have to be stale, boring, or a deadbeat in bed.

- A gentleman is charismatic and is self-confident.

- He is able to express his feelings freely and respectfully.

- Gentleman look for ways to boost a woman's self-esteem.

Typically bad boys fall into three categories:

Natural Born: They are born that way, and will never be anything more than a jerk.

Jilted Lovers: The second group is suffering from the heartbreak of a broken romance. Burned by a bad relationship, these guys are the walking wounded. This jerk will use abusive means to keep women away.

Low Self-Esteem: Sadly, this man has to act like a jerk to disguise his lack of confidence. His snide remarks and sarcasm are used as defense mechanisms, kind of how a skunk releases a stench to ward off those who may be a threat.

- A jerk uses crude, sarcastic, and vulgar language.

- A jerk is often rude or arrogant in public.

- Jerks give the illusion of strength, but lack the substance of true leadership.

- His behavior is random and sometimes reckless.

Why Do Woman Fall For Jerks?

A major difference between a gentleman and a jerk is self-esteem. In the beginning of a relationship, he looks like a strong protective alpha male. Women find jerks attractive because he projects a certain level of confidence. His aggression gives her a sense of protection and security. These men can be very powerful. Gentleman are strong, assertive, and in control of their emotions. A jerk may be strong, successful, and assertive, but his low self-esteem causes him to lose control of his emotions.

Confident women who have experience with men can quickly spot a jerk. She will identify his immature, toxic ways and get out of the relationship. Women that are more dependent and have low self-esteem tend to get trapped. The relationship quickly degrades into an abusive situation. She complains about what a terrible guy he is, but seems helpless to leave his grasp. Because they both have very low self-esteem, they make a perfect match—a perfectly miserable match.

Some women have a savior complex. These wannabe relationship therapists feel that it is their biological duty to fix their men. Women love to know that they're the ones who discovered the solution to their boyfriend's problems and, in turn, healed them. He was once a bad boy, but now he is a sweetheart and he's a changed man, all thanks to her. Yes, this is the challenge most women enjoy seeking, an incredible feat where they claim to have turned a lost soul around. If a man was perfect to begin with, what would be so exciting in the relationship?

In the beginning of the relationship, she knew that he had a few rough edges, but in time she could whip him into shape. Regardless of what she does, he simply does not understand or care that his behavior is poisoning the relationship. This guy does not value the relationship enough to alter his personality. He could be on the rebound from a bad relationship, and therefore understandingly uncomfortable with deep commitment. He might be the type of person that simply does not see the value of a substantial relationship. It does not mean that he is a bad person or there is something wrong with him. He is not broken, simply unable or unwilling to change for you.

Frustrated Frieda

Unfortunately, there are a group of women who never seem to be able to accept the man in their relationship. They continue to insist, demand, cajole, or use any manipulating technique at their disposal to change their significant other. She is mistakenly motivated by a misguided understanding of love, believing that she has to do whatever it takes '*in the name of love*' to make the relationship work. In her drive to succeed at love, she forgot that it takes two people to be in a relationship. Ultimately, they will drive the man right out of their relationship. Once the man leaves, she becomes bitter and unbearable to deal with. I like to think of these ladies as *Frustrated Frieda's*.

Rescuing Frieda

Most of us have been unwilling participants of a Frustrated Frieda relationship rescue. Typically, it starts with the tearful, desperate late night phone call. *"Hey Girl, this is Frieda. You got a minute? I had to get rid of that jerk! He just would not get with the program."* Against your better instincts, you respond with *"…Frieda, what happened?"* For the next couple of hours she replays the relationship—he did this, he did that, *blah, blah, blah!* Frieda goes on to tell you that she did everything for that guy. She even apologizes for ignoring your advice and nearly ruining your friendship. Frieda is truly devastated and needs the help. Unfortunately, Frieda never openly takes any credit for the failure of the relationship.

As you listen to Frieda do an emotional toilet flush on the broken relationship, you quickly realize that she has a more serious problem than the occasional bad relationship. She does not know when to relax, to live and let live.

Most relationships will eventually settle at a healthy level where there is mutual respect and acceptance. Frustrated Frieda's will never reach the point of respect and acceptance. They are too busy denying and demanding. She denies the current reality of her relationship. The reality that her mate has certain behaviors that have always been there, like snoring or watching internet porn. Rather than recognize his unwillingness to change, she pushes and pushes until he leaves the relationship.

Key Takeaways

1. ***There is no Such Thing as a Broken Man!*** Simply because your personality is not compatible with the man of your dreams does not mean that he is broken. He is just not right for you.

2. ***Understand Yourself!*** The first step to correcting a problem, emotional or otherwise, is to recognize you have a problem. '*You can't change what you don't acknowledge.*' Do you know what it is that makes you happy? Take an inventory of your emotions.

3. ***Like Yourself!*** If you don't like the person in the mirror, how can you expect anyone else to like them? Become comfortable with who you are.

4. ***Be Responsible!*** You are responsible for your own happiness.

5. ***He is a Guy!*** Men and women are wired differently. As such, their goals in a relationship are different. That is neither good nor bad, just different.

6. ***Accept the Natural Change!*** There is a natural movement to any relationship. Sometimes it moves her way other times his way. A woman can encourage change with patience, love, and kindness. Forcing change often leads to destruction of the relationship.

7. ***Let Him Decide to Change!*** If a man wants change, he will. The minute she starts telling him what to do is when he stops being her man and starts being her child.

8. ***Let Him Have Space!*** If he enjoys spending time in the man cave working on cars or building computers, let him have that space. He in turn will respect you and make the time you spend together more meaningful.

Can You Really Fix a Bad Boy?

In the beginning of the relationship, she knew that he had a few rough edges, but in time she could whip him into shape. Regardless of what she does, he simply does not understand or care that his behavior is poisoning the relationship. This guy is not ready for a serious relationship, or he does not value the relationship enough to alter his personality. It does not mean that he is a bad person or there is something wrong with him. He is not broken, simply unable or unwilling to change for you.

Recommended Readings

Emotional Bailout – Nine Principles For Rising When Your World Is Falling by Cathy Holloway Hill

Dear Lover – A Woman's Guide To Men, Sex, And Love's Deepest Bliss by David Deida

Drama Kings – The Men Who Drive Strong Women Crazy by Dalma Heyn

Notes:

ABOUT THE AUTHOR

REV. DARLENE ROBINSON

Rev. Darlene Robinson is an Elder in the East Ohio Conference of the United Methodist Church. She is a native of Youngstown, Ohio. She graduated high school in 1978 from The Rayen School where she earned the esteemed honor of being class Valedictorian. Darlene was given a standing ovation after completion of her Valedictorian speech. Rev. Robinson graduated from Malone College in Canton, Ohio in 1990 with a Bachelor of Arts degree in Management.

Following a call from God upon her life, Darlene pursued a seminary degree and during those years she was recognized as a Crusade Scholar of the United Methodist Church by the General Board of Global Ministries in 1997. Rev. Robinson graduated from Ashland Theological Seminary, Ashland, Ohio in 2001 with a Master of Divinity degree. She was given the Spiritual Formation award for the Cleveland Campus of Ashland Seminary also in 2001. Darlene is a member of the Professional Woman Network (PWN), the Network of Biblical Storytellers and the Cleveland Association of Black Storytellers (CABS). Rev. Robinson was married to the late Rev. Dr. Dennis Alexander Robinson for 21 years. They were blessed with three sons, Dasan, David and Dennis Albert. Her mother, Emma Robinson, also resides in her home.

She began her pastoral ministry with an interim appointment during the summer of 2001 at Vincent United Methodist Church in Elyria, Ohio. She was then appointed in September of 2001 to serve in a shared ministry as the pastor of 2 churches in Lorain, Ohio. Their names were Faith and Emmanuel United Methodist Churches. She remained at both churches until 2008 when the Emmanuel church merged with two other United Methodist Churches within the city of Lorain. In addition to pastoring the Faith Church, she then became one of three pastors on staff at the newly merged Lighthouse United Methodist Church. Rev. Robinson served full time as pastor to Cove United Methodist Church in Lakewood, Ohio which began in July of 2008. She is currently in another shared ministry as the pastor of both Cove United Methodist Church and at Fairview Grace United Methodist Church in Fairview Park, Ohio. She was appointed to Fairview Grace in July 2009. Darlene and her family currently reside in Elyria, Ohio.

Contact:
Business Address: P.O. Box 761, Elyria, OH 44036
Telephone: 440-506-7773 cell
Email: Darden7@msn.com
Website Address: www.Darlene-Robinson.webs.com

TWENTY-FOUR

ENCOURAGEMENT

By Darlene Robinson

I have a friend that works for a funeral home. This person will occasionally converse with me about the deceased persons that are brought to the funeral home. My friend will sometimes tell me the person's age and how they died. I have been most surprised at the number of people who have passed away because of suicide…death at their own hands. Their ages vary. My middle son also has a friend whose mother attempted suicide recently, as well. Thank God she did not succeed. Her rationale for doing so was that she felt like she was not a good mother. I am not sure what that statement entailed in terms of her thinking and processing at the time. I can tell you this though, somewhere down the line in her life she must have entered into some form of discouragement.

Discouragement, like a heavy dark cloud moving across the sky, can overtake any of us at any time during our lifetime. It can bring on depression like a thick fog settling upon the earth. You get to the place where you can't see life clearly anymore. You lose your direction. You slow down almost to a crawl or you end up stopping all together, possibly spending many days or too much time in bed depressed. You may end up on the couch curled up in the fetal position, wrapped up in a blanket feeling sad, not engaging life head on, not taking care of your responsibilities and not experiencing the joy that living can bring. Now don't get me wrong. I don't want to seem like I am too critical about those who end up in this situation because I have at times over the years ended up experiencing bouts with discouragement as well over various situations and circumstances in my life. I, too, have been bruised with issues that cause discouragement. But thank God I have not been broken into a zillion pieces, although sometimes it felt like I had. There are many women who have been bruised because of their life experiences. Some have been physically abused and bruises have been left on their bodies as reminders of the terror they experienced. Discouragement "bruising" can come from verbal abuse. Relationships "gone bad" are also causes of bruising. In my pastoral and life experiences, I have found that these relationships "gone bad" could happen between a husband and wife, boyfriend and girlfriend, parent and child, employer and employee, friend and friend and others. Experiencing grief, loneliness, heartache, heartbreak, shock, trauma, disappointment with how life has turned out, disappointment with yourself and your choices and even dare I say, disappointment with God are also situations that can cause discouragement.

One can also become discouraged because of a lack of a relationship(s) in your life, such as the lack of a boyfriend, husband, child, parent or even a real good honest trustworthy friend. Yes, bruising by discouragement occurs more often in our lives than we are willing to sometimes admit. The pain and bruising of discouragement can come to all.

So how does one endure and come through the bruising of discouragement? Here is a scripture that I have found that will save many of you thousands of dollars in unnecessary health costs due to the ill health that one might have fallen into because of discouragement and depression. The scripture says in John 16: 33, *"I have told you this so that through me you may have peace. In the world **you will** have trouble, but be courageous. I have overcome the world!"*—International Standard Version(©2008)

Jesus is saying here as I paraphrase, "Listen everyone, let me tell you about the world in which you live. It is a world in which you will experience the lack of peace in your life. I can give you the peace you need, and you will need it. In this world you will have problems and troubles. This is a given. You will…you will…you will have problems!!!! This is going to be a part of life and living. So don't go "tripping" every time something happens. Things are going to happen. Let me repeat this, *things are going to happen.* Stop acting so surprised when trouble comes. Stop beating yourself up about life happening, especially if you feel like you don't deserve the trouble that comes your way. The only place where things are going to be perfect will be in heaven and you have not made it their yet. So until then, take courage, be courageous, and take heart. Why? It is because I have overcome the world. I win in the end!!!!! And guess what? You will win also if you just don't give up."

Question:

Now that you know that problems are a part of life, how does this passage of scripture make you feel?

I believe that God can use every situation that we go through to teach us something about life and about ourselves. These lessons or teachable moments can all eventually be turned into something good. Romans 8:28 (New Living Translation) says, *"And we know that God causes everything to work together for the good of those who love God and are called according to his purpose for them."*

The experience that we have gone through may not be good. No, nothing good about it at all. The experience may have been terrifying and excruciatingly painful. Some experiences that we go through may also come from our own mistakes, bad decisions and out of control desires. However, God has the ability to carry us through these and all experiences and lead us to healing and wholeness so that we can continue on in life victoriously. Yes, it is true that we may have to suffer the consequences of our actions, but we still can make it through life victoriously if we reach out for help.

Question:

Who or what do you reach out to during your time of crisis?

_____

Has this reaching out been helpful or harmful? If harmful, what changes do you need to make in terms of who/what you reach out to for help?

_____

_____

When going through discouragement, we need to stop and ask ourselves some of the following questions:

Why am I discouraged?

Is it one single event or several situations?

Is it just your dissatisfaction with where you are in life?

(You also may not know what is causing these feelings. In this case, some professional counseling may be needed, especially if suicidal or homicidal thoughts pervade your mind.)

In regards to suicide, I have often shared with my three sons that no matter how bad life gets, suicide is never an option. God can work out any situation in our lives no matter how terrible it is. Yes, this is easier said than done, but it is true. There are many testimonies from persons who have endured awful things and survived and have come through victoriously at the other end. Did they suffer hurt and pain? Yes, for the most part, but God was able to carry them through.

I have tried to convey to my sons, especially in regards to their girlfriend relationships, that their hearts may get broken but suicide and/or homicide is not the option to alleviating their pain. It is my hope and prayer that they will continue to remember this message. I told them, as I am sharing with you, to not get caught up in the songs or music that they listen to that have lyrics that say words like, *I just can't live without you, I just can't make it without you, I won't breath again if you are not in my life,* **or** *I would rather be dead and in my grave than be without you.*

Well, break-ups and a loss by death of a loved one that you are in a relationship with are excruciatingly painful and sometimes debilitating but…but….but….my friend, with God's help you can get through the other side of the break-up and the grief. You may be scarred. You may be bruised. You may have a limp. You may never be the same. However, you can get through and go on and live victoriously and you can and will survive.

I know of at least one person that actually attempted suicide and another person who had a relative that attempted to kill herself over a break-up. In the case of the person that I know, she told me that a nurse in the hospital talked some sense into her and she vowed never to try that again. In the case of my friend whose relative attempted suicide, he told me that he and his girlfriend at the time were able to help her see that suicide is not the way to solve a break-up. So does this really happen? Yes, my friend it does.

Break-ups, loss by death, loss by other means, as well as being in situations that involve our emotions and intimacy can happen at any age now. Marriages are breaking up after 20, 30 and 40+ years. Spouses and/or significant others are breaking up and/or dying after couples have been together for years. Women now in their 30's, 40's, 50's and up are dealing with such issues as heart ache and pain. If you don't believe me, just watch the show, "Divorce Court" and read your local newspaper. Discouragement can become a part of a person's life at any age.

Aging issues also become real and can cause lapses into depression. Especially when you realize that you may be losing your independence. You may be losing your youthful looks and your perceived beauty seems to be fleeing. Your remaining years at this end of your life are getting shorter than they were when you were in your teens and twenties. If single, your chances for a future mate may appear to be slim or non-existent. Discouragement about the future begins to set it.

Question:

What is the lesson that I should be learning in this discouragement situation and during this time?

_____

What is my appropriate response?

_____

Is this something I caused?

_____

Is there something that I can do to rectify the situation?

_____

If the answer to the last question is yes, then get on it. Do your best, if possible, to rectify the situation or make it better. If not, then realize that there is nothing you can do about it, pray and move on. Go as far as you can to check and double check that there is nothing more you can do. Also, realize that it may be your calling now to help others in a similar situation to make it through or to keep from making the same mistake(s) that you may or someone else may have made. Many foundations, charities, scholarships and other programs or ministries have been started based upon someone's tragedy and how they or their families have tried to find ways to help others.

Question:
- Is there something in your life that needs to be rearranged or reprioritized?

- What steps do you need to take to make this happen?

- Is this something God would approve of?

- Would this decision cause too much harm or endanger someone?

- What ways can you now help those who find themselves in a similar situation(s) as yours?

Here are some practical ideas as to how you may help yourself out of *discouragement lane* **and be on your way to** *encouragement place***:**

1. Remembering that Life = 10% of what happens to you + 90% of how you handle the things that happen to you.

2. Think about how far you have already come in life and think that today is just **one** not so great of a day.

3. Know that God is in control.

4. No matter how bad you have it, somebody may have it worse.

5. Think "Don't worry be happy" like Bobby McFerrin sings.

6. Look at the biblical character Job. He went through several tragedies but he continued to trust God and God eventually restored to him double of what he had lost.

7. Make music.

8. Pray.

9. Get up and get ready for the day.

10. Listen to gospel music.

11. Read your Bible.

12. Just wait and the fog will clear.

13. Get professional counseling.

14. Give back to others.

15. Teach Sunday School.

16. Volunteer at a hospital or school.

17. Laugh and talk with others.

18. Interview other people to find out their life story.

19. Take the focus off of you.

20. Listen to jokes.

21. Tell jokes.

22. Make people laugh.

23. Enjoy being around family.

24. Help people.

25. Count your blessings.

26. Being thankful.

27. Realize that sometimes there is nothing that you can do about a situation.

28. Keep on pushing.

29. Take one day at a time.

30. Learn to let things roll off your back.

31. Pick and choose your battles.

32. Ask God about His will being done.

33. Love people.

34. Love God.

35. Play games.

36. Spend time with family.

37. Travel.

38. Go help those who are less fortunate.

39. Realize that each day is a gift of God.

40. Remember that trouble doesn't last always.

41. Take the mandatory eight count and get up swinging (like in boxing).

42. Take a walk.

43. Go for a drive.

44. Visit or call encouraging family members.

45. Visit or call encouraging friends.

46. Enjoy the sunshine.

47. Look at the moon.

48. Cook and eat a healthy meal.

49. Exercise.

50. Don't just sit there, do something!

Be Encouraged

My heart is heavy, my spirit is low,
So much that I don't know which way to go.
The pain I feel is so unbelievably real
It makes me want to take another anti-depressant pill.
A pill to numb my feelings so the pain will go away,
But all it does is come back another day.
Or maybe instead of a pill, I will reach for something to eat,
Something greasy, fattening, sugary and sweet.
It only makes me seem happy for a little while
But soon after, the high blood sugar wears away my smile.
My soul aches for something new,
But all I experience is the feeling of being blue.
I want to reach out but the depression is so thick;
Love, peace and joy have evaded me and now I am sick.

So sick with sadness and sorrow
It seems like I have no hope of tomorrow.
I've been beat down by the world in which I live
So that I have no desire for anyone my love to give.
Some mistakes are because of what I have done;
Now life for me doesn't hold much fun.
Bruised by abuse, Bruised by life, Bruised by pain
But Be encouraged my friend and don't live in the mundane.
But broken I am not, and broken I will not be
For I have the Creator within me.
Yes, sometimes I get down and low;
Discouragement seems the only way to go.
But I get encouraged from Him up above,
God is the one who gives me genuine love.
It is because of His love that I can now clearly see
That the fog of discouragement was sent to destroy me.
But I won't, I can't, I just can't let it get me down anymore
Because God has so much in life for me in store.
A life filled with joy and happiness down to my core.
I'm in the fight for my life, I'm declaring war.
Tears will no longer control;
I will use them to strengthen my soul.
Why do I worry, why do I fret
When God is in control, my life is set.
So be encouraged my friend
All the way to life's end.
Even when you make the wrong choices
And listen to the wrong voices.
Learn from your error and move on;

Be encouraged and be strong.
Find your strength in the things that God provides.
You will be surprised at the pleasures He hides
In simple things and wonderful people.
So go ahead and spend some time under that church steeple.
Be encouraged my friend,
Your trouble will one day end.
This too shall pass as it is said.
So keep all these good words in your head.
Soon you will be on your way to loving again
And knowing that in life with God you can really win.
—An Original Poem by Darlene Robinson

ABOUT THE AUTHOR

NERLIE PIERRE CLARK, MS/MFT

Mrs. Nerlie Pierre Clark is the President and CEO of *Pierre Clark and Associates, International* (PCAI) consulting firm. Based in Philadelphia, Pennsylvania, PCAI is purposed to draw professionalism from passion. PCAI works via professional development strategies to equip employees of the health, judicial, educational, non-profit and faith-based arenas towards best service practices of clientele composed predominantly of children and their families. PCAI pushes organizations to reach beyond passion for their work to perfection in service. PCAI fields of expertise include:

Diversity & Consumer Relations
Leadership Development
Parent & Youth Advocacy
Team Productivity & Management
Training & Development for Educators/Providers
Culture & Gender Awareness
Effective Communication
Time Management
Program Development
Curriculum Development
Women & Youth Ministries
Dove Self-Esteem Workshops
Self Empowerment & Wellness

Mrs. Clark is a motivated professional with 7+ years of project management and process improvement experience in the non-profit, local government, and mental health industries. Proven leader who has directed and managed professionals to significant improvements in productivity and performance and families to achieving their full potential. Following her Ivy League undergraduate education from the University of Pennsylvania (Philadelphia, PA), she attained her Masters in Counseling and Clinical Psychology in Marriage and Family Therapy at Chestnut Hill College (Philadelphia, PA), and is currently pursuing her doctorate in Psychology (Couple and Family Therapy) at Drexel University (Philadelphia, PA).

Mrs. Clark is married to wonderful man of God and they worked tirelessly in support of their pastor and church congregation in ministry. They also founded the *Family Leadership and Empowerment Institute* non-profit that seeks to revive the concept, meaning and healthy functioning of the family. It does this by facilitating and providing full range leadership support and mentoring for all families through social development, marriage and family therapy, mentoring relationships, social service support, and youth development. Currently, FLEI is focusing its efforts on the homeless population in Philadelphia, PA with training and development workshops, advocacy and community service.

Contact:
Pierre Clark & Associates, International (PCAI)
P.O. Box 18886
Philadelphia, PA 19119
Phone: 215-520-1244, Email:PCAIConsulting@gmail.com
Website:www.pcaiconsulting.com
Follow us on: Facebook, Twitter, In and YouTube

TWENTY-FIVE

THE AWESOME WRUSH OF HEALTHY RELATIONSHIPS

By Nerlie Pierre Clark

My husband and I had been snorkeling off the coast of Montego Bay in Jamaica recently. On one occasion, the weather condition was so windy that the captain cautioned us to be hyper vigilant of our location in the water, as the wind caused stronger waves than normal and greatly increased the water's velocity. Determined to absorb as much from the Caribbean experience as possible, we jumped into the water and continued our exploration of the sea's majestic beauty, despite the caution.

Within minutes, we recognized the increased hardship lurking the waters, yet hoped to appropriately navigating through its folds. Unusually, the waves propelled us forward from the boat as we equipped ourselves for the mission.

"Ouch! Gasp! Ick!" we exclaimed as the waves came *rushing* salt water against our masks and into or eyes and nostrils, then clogging our snorkeling tubes and into our mouths. Defeated, I made way back to the boat and my mini excavation came to a premature end. "Wow, the awesome *rush* of wind and waves!" I pondered.

Even today, I linger in the stupor of the pair's strength. Just a day before I was unstoppable. Did the wind, or did the sea alone halt my progression? I proceeded in a solid cohort of flotation device, fins and snorkeling gear. I assumed that this equipment would be just right for any condition in the water, but I was mistaken. This day, the wind and waves joined becoming an invincible force that all this equipment was now too weak to protect me against. I (as an external and unnatural being of the sea) was unable to further invade and violate its majestic innocence through a make-shift breathing device and manufactured fins that once permitted me to imitate a genuine member of its sincere body.

Quickly, I awakened to the notion that God didn't bless me with gills, and on a windy day, I *need* to keep myself on the land where I belong! I furthermore recognized that I could not withstand the turbulent movement as much as a genuine entity of the sea could. I assure you that the blue damsel fish swimming beneath me did not follow me into the boat. It was not at all hindered or negatively affected by the pair's turbulence. The fish depend on the movement, consistency and nature of the water for survival. It willingly went with the flow, but I pushed against it. The advancement of the water equals the advancement of the fish.

Such is the relationships we form in life. Healthy relationships are associations that correspond. The individuals in healthy partnerships overlap in their likes, dislikes, beliefs, interests, affiliations and/or family ties. Relationships are often formed stemming from these areas of similarity and they rely on each other for support, encouragement, and progression. The wind, water and fish work together in this manner. I did not share beneficial abilities with the trio. Remaining impotent in this territory would ultimately be to my detriment. Sometimes we remain in relationships in which we do not share commonalities with others or bonds in which our skills or abilities do not coincide. This renders us powerless. However, if we would be awakened to our rightful purpose in life and collaborate with others that share this purpose, we could arrive to the magnificence and strength of the trio that we experienced that day in Jamaica.

The healthy relationship between two individuals in an element in which they rightfully operate produces such *rush* and forward movement that it rids itself of any faulty matter that did not support, contribute to or fall in line with its flow. It didn't matter the swimming skills or equipment that I had to imitate water beings. When a mighty rush challenged my very sense of what life was, I had no choice but to return to my elite territory of operation – the land. Whether it be a collaboration formed because of the purpose of seeking joy in life or a collaboration because of a huge business venture. When people join in commonality of purpose, they are strengthened and become a force to be reckoned with.

Health can be recognized as a phenomenon that is of *superhuman* quality. It requires a strategic collaboration of both internal and external entities that promotes life, movement and growth. The sea alone in its grandeur did not have the ability to repel us from its bank, nor could the wind distract us alone during our sail. However, when the two joined in collaboration, it became a strong force that stopped me dead in my tracks. If I decided to ignore the message telling me that I did not belong there, it could have costs me my life. There are times in life in which life sends us clear messages signaling us back to our elite territories of prime functioning—our purpose—in order to function in life at our highest potential. Are we making our way back to the boat or ignoring the messages? If we choose to ignore the message, we may very soon be bruised or even drown in a territory in which we were never destined to exist.

As in the collaboration of the wind, water and the fish of the sea, individuals in healthy relationships each play a distinct role. Select duties contribute to the overall greatness of the unit. The stronger the bond is, the more powerful the unit becomes, which then equals the power of its individual members. We should not form relationships to show our own strength over the other (this is what occurs in abusive relationships), but rather we should form relationships with another with a purpose to compliment and to be complimented. This will produce growth and strength.

Healthy Relationships That Will Protect You in the Bruised State

Relationship is "a connection, association, or involvement." It is "an aspect or quality (as resemblance) that connects two or more things or parts as being or belonging or working together or as being of the same kind." Thus, the term refers to a joining of corresponding entities functioning coherently or in a uniformed manner. The relationships that we form with others should primarily be founded on commonality. The saying "opposites attract" only references one aspect of the relationship spectrum. Even in considering the opposite ends of two magnets joining, you must first recognize that the two being joined have a common linkage: they are both magnets. The differences between one person to another cannot not be found in the foundation and linkage of the individual elements being joined, for an orange will not connect to a magnet no matter what end you link it to. Therefore, our relationships must be founded on semblance.

Health is "the condition of being sound in body, mind, or spirit; especially freedom from physical disease or pain" Being "healthy" refers to the *enjoyment* of health and the vigor of body, mind and spirit. Health, in fact, emanates a glow of prosperity and flourish that presents as what I refer to as a **WRUSH**:

Wholesome: implies appearance and behavior indicating soundness and balance

Robust: implies the opposite of all that is delicate or sickly

Useful: being of use or service; serving some purpose, producing material results

Sound: emphasizes the absence of weakness, or malfunction

Hale: applies particularly to robustness in old age, strong, well-conditioned

In **WRUSH Relationship** with the wind, the sea was propelled to an ultimate level of movement—a rush. What internal and external partnerships and relationships are WRUSH towards your rush? A WRUSH Relationship is conditioned to allow us to simultaneously impact and be impacted by others. That day, the sea was enhanced to a level of strength by the push of the wind and its acceptance of external impact allowed it now to become a push for the living in it.

In WRUSH Relationships, there are expected levels of initiative and compliance that is required to keep the coalition alive and moving. The longer the coalition lasts, the more endurance they develop, and the stronger it becomes. The strategic alignment of both internal and external elements that form relationships is what I call the **WRUSHing Self.**

Attaining the WRUSHing Self can be likened to the rushing movement of the water in the sea that day, as it was undeniably strong, resistant and advancive, that it literally evaded itself of any inauthentic, contaminating, opposing or alien matter. It is an internal process requiring the self to form a relationship with the self. Achievement of the WRUSHing Self causes one to disconnect from and relinquish ideals, thoughts, decisions, or people that are inauthentic (untruthful to the true self), contaminating (bruising to the self), opposing (contrary to the self), or alien (unfamiliar to the self). It requires profound introspection. Your *self* deserves truth. Your *self* deserves care. Your *self* deserves support. Your *self* deserves harmony that will render it to be ultimately strong, resistant and advancive of its own existence and purpose.

It is not until the *WRUSHing Self* is achieved that we can look to pursuing a *WRUSHing Relationship* with others, for the "connection, association, or involvement" with others, requires that we are aware of who we are before we could extend an invitation to another in affiliation. Do you wait until your living room is the messiest to invite a guest into your home? Of course not. So why do we often invite others to befriend us, partner in business or fall in love with us, when we are feeling the most "all over the place?" No one desires to befriend a leech. It's a person who I define as one who always wants and takes without giving anything in return. Hitching a ride in life as a parasite will get us what we want temporarily, but one day we will be discovered and plucked off. Where will we be then? Nowhere.

Recovery from the Bruised State

The "Bruised State" is a state of danger. Not only is it a condition in which one experiences much pain, but it is also a condition in which one is most vulnerable and impressionable. Intimate consorts with others draw us to begin to trust others with our thoughts, emotions and our authentic self. When others betray that trust, that rash disappointment of our hope and expectation of their loyalty often ignites anguish. This response is indeed warranted, yet its persistence can be quite debilitating. One of the major mistakes that we make is not allowing ourselves time to grieve this loss of affiliation and the bruise that forms afterward. There are healthy methods in which we can grieve the loss of a relationship, such as therapy, prayer and most importantly forgiveness. Engaging in a form of emotional processing does not promise a quick fix, rather it guides us to appropriately feel and adjust as we move on.

The Power of Forgiveness

Forgiveness is a decision to cease resentment against another. The refusal to forgive another for an infraction on us is a choice that we make that ultimately hinders the healing of a bruise. Let's consider this: As is a physical bruise, emotional or psychological bruises are visible. Overtime in appropriate circumstances, bruises fade away and heal. The persistent appearance of a bruise evidences two possibilities that indicate that there is:

1. Active injury to the bruise is present, or

2. Abnormal functioning of the internal healing mechanism

While the first figuratively alludes to the active persistence of a bruising relationship, the latter represents what is occurring in us when we fail to forgive others. When we refuse to forgive, it is an internal abnormality that portrays a bruised image to the world. In this state, a person may behave in a withdrawn manner and the minimal interactions that s(he) may have with other people may be harsh or aggressive in manner. This person behaves in this way often because of the pain that lurks within them, so they remain on the defense to resist further bruising. However, as a perpetual physical bruise can produce blood clots that are dangerous to our health, or even fatal, so the emotional, spiritual and psychological nature can lead to such death. Forgiveness is imperative, for it is much more a benefit to us than it is to the other person. It is utter deliverance, freedom from emotional, spiritual and psychological bondage, and is genuine healing that allows us to feel again...connect again...live again.

The Significance of Differentiation

Some find it difficult to forgive because they have given so much of themselves (mostly unwillingly) that they have nothing left and begin to rely on the existence of a relationship with others for survival. In most instances, they are no longer able to distinguish their own will from that of the others. This is referred to as fusion. Forgiveness does not work with a person that is fused with another. It requires a habitually powerless and fearful individual (hence why they rely on a relationship with another to survive) to do something that they have never been able to do before—to face themselves. In order to forgive and have a new or altered start, we must face ourselves, and make the adjustments necessary to protect ourselves from a repeated offense.

The process towards correcting a fused relationship is called differentiation. Differentiation is the process in which one becomes distinct or different in character from another. It is a formulation of individual identity from those around us (such as family members, co-workers, fellow congregants, etc.). The concept of Differentiation of Self was developed by Dr. Murray Bowen (1913-1990) who worked rigorously towards the science of human behavior as a scholar, clinician, researcher, teacher and writer. His depiction of the term says that a person whose self is not well-defined is who will seek control of or will be controlled by others. What is your role in respect to those around you? What is your identity? Although we share the genes with a biological family member, it is our responsibility to merge both natural and environmental factor to form our own sense of being and character. When we know who we are, it forms our standard that makes us less impressionable to outside influence. It then becomes our measuring stick of acceptance or refusal of mannerisms, thoughts, affiliation, or beliefs that meet our standard and level of self. WRUSH relationships are those that meet and encourage our standards of existence, health and purpose.

Adjusting to Isolation and Identity Formation

Prior to a necessity for this stage, we interacted with the world through our defined roles with our family and those around them (see figure 1). We saw the self simply as the daughter/son, sister/brother, and so on of another person. Isolation draws us to a deeper level of self. The process in which one defines and establishes his identity will require moments of isolation. This may (or may not) refer to a literal separation from current friends and associates and even family members. It is a complete diversion of external distractions that draws you into purposeful focus. Isolation coerces us to do one crucial deed: face our self in a bare and vulnerable state. Commonly, the need for isolation comes when we feel a loosened grasp of the people, things and circumstances about us, or have been bruised from the failure of past relationship with people, places, or things. If we consider adventure on the sea symbolically, it is the time in which the water rushes against us, cautioning our pursuance of a danger zone and to return to safety on the boat. We must attend to life's warnings and return to safety so that we avoid being swallowed up by the waves of life. To many us, this presents as an arduous and frightening task. The man in the mirror reveals our most personal and uncommon qualities. Before then, most of us have spent our entire lives searching for how we can fit in with other people instead of how other people can fit in with who we are. Isolation removes distraction from the unattainable standards that others place, permitting us to form our own standards that consider our abilities, beliefs and exceptional qualities that we each bring to the world.

OTHERS

FAMILY

SELF

Following our birth, we acquire our connection to the world via our natural senses. Our senses are raging in development as we establish our first sense of sight, taste, smell, sound and touch of the world that surrounds us. Our family works to nurture us and teach us how to maneuver our senses to interact with the world. Thus, our most primitive conceptualization of our self is learned from the family. Based solely on normal brain development, this occurs approximately from birth to the early 20's.

Let us consider the human body: Void of understanding of its purpose of functioning, the human nose will begin to covet the functioning of other features on the face. It may start to detest itself because it realizes that it is unable to benefit the body with sight like the eyes can, or sound as can the ears. However, you and I both can appreciate the value of the nose when it gets stuffy and we lose our sense of taste. It becomes difficult to enjoy a meal, or absorb the sweet smelling baking of chocolate chip cookies in the oven, or to detect the dangerous emergence of a fire without the nose. If the nose remains unaware of its purpose in functioning, its existence revolves around an ever yearning to be like others, a void in appropriate functioning and an eventual failure of the body. We, too, can fail life if we waste life in the ignorance of our purpose in function. In prevention of such failure arises the need for self-definition of identity through profound research, study and meditation of your physical and spiritual lineage, purpose and abilities.

Success in profound introspection requires the consideration of 4 points:

1. **The Will of God** – As referenced in the book of *Jeremiah* 29:11 in the Holy Bible, God knows the plans that He has for us. We must

go to the source of life to know how to live. In God's word we find detailed and intimate instruction to living an abundant life. Most importantly, we find the Creator face-to-face in continual prayer in our quest for guidance and a revelation of what He has manufactured as our purposed function.

2. **Our Gifts and Capabilities** – Our skills and talents serve as indicators towards our field(s) of maximum impact. We have unique traits and abilities that are innate that serve as life road signs regulating our intended direction and speed towards living in purpose.

3. **Our Life Purpose** – There are spiritual and physical purposes to life, and defining them requires a combination of points 1and 2. Our defined purpose serves as a standard marking what we can or cannot do and draws us to exclusivity, distinction and specialty.

4. **Relevant Goal Planning** – This is the action period. Knowledge of points 1-3 are idle without action. Forming a list of relevant goals with realistic timelines and following through is crucial to living in purpose. A structured and detailed plan of action serves as a checking point and reiteration of the overall objective as we proceed through the intermediate goals prior to the finish line.

The period of isolation varies from one person to another. However, it is a time requiring the courage to be honest with oneself, prayer, strategic planning and patience. In today's world, we place much emphasis on the investment of our time, money, talents and skills into external factors so that we may reap of them. Yet, the most rewarding of what we can experience in this lifetime is that which we invest into ourselves according to our divine purpose so that we ultimately sow into the lives of those around us. As selfish as it may seem at the onset, the period of isolation is a time in which we learn who we are and who's we are towards improving the lives that surround us.

WRUSH Relationships Don't Bruise
Understanding Purpose of Relationship with Others

Following our recalibration of identity and purpose, we must collaborate with others. There is no way to avoid relationship, for we are created as relational beings. From the point of birth, our sustenance relies on a collaboration of our innate senses with external partnerships. To survive and attain success, relationships must be formed with others to support our functioning and overall purpose. Often, we hesitate to collaborate with others as a result of fear and shame that may manifest as:

- Fear of being bruised again

- Fear of ridicule or disbelief

- Fear of the unknown

- Shame of past experiences or actions

Forming healthy relationships with others serves to protect, promote and progress the predestined existence of all members of that body. Remember that, in a body, in order for all members to achieve this level, they rarely serve the same function. Conflict arises when members fight for the same recognition. Healthy relationships are such that even if the action of a member is temporarily halted or unrecognized, protection, promotion and progression is still realized via the achievement of another. Through life's storms along our path to purpose, we need encouragement to persevere. Sometimes we will need a reminder towards our established standard so that we can protect against imitators and intruders that seek to halt our progression. Our spiritual, personal, business, familial, platonic or romantic relationships should be formed with those who can challenge us to remain faithful to our goal, humble enough to comply our function in purpose, yet established enough to lead in their own purpose. This produces dependability, trust and lifelong friendship.

Preparation for Re-Acquaintance with Others

Shame from the past and fear of the future are not valid excuses for stagnancy! When these emotions arise, we should give ourselves time to identify and process them prior to forming new relationships. While it is important to receive consolation and counsel from others at times, it is more important to face the emotions and process them independently. Preparing to collaborate with others in relationship requires us to keep our purpose in mind as a standard and to be strong enough to do the same for a counterpart. The WRUSH Relationship is formed with careful intent (see figure 2). Those in which an alliance is formed must not only support our growth, but we also need to support theirs. A good friend will give us what s(he) has, but most importantly give us what s(he) gives him/herself. Take a good look at the friends that you have now. What are they giving themselves? Is it love, truth and encouragement or is it hatred, lies and destruction? This will indicate what they will render you in friendship, for they cannot give you what they do not have.

GOD

SELF

OTHERS

PLATONIC RELATIONSHIP

FAMILY RELATIONSHIP

LIFE PURPOSE

Following late adolescence and into early adulthood, we should begin transitioning from a relationship to the world via the family, to a direct connection from the self to the world that now consists of relationships both internal and external to the formal family structure. Also, we begin to acquire a sense of which relationships and associations are most beneficial to developing who we are and encouraging our progress to God's spiritual and physical purposes for us.

Identifying an Un-WRUSH Relationship

An unhealthy relationship is recognized as one that seeks to destroy us. It can manifest apparently as in a physically abusive relationship or more subtly in the form of usury. It does not serve to build us up, but instead, its intent is to break us down so that it is lifted up over us. That is NOT healthy relationship.

An un-WRUSH Relationship is the OPPOSITE of:

- **un-W**holesome: implies the *lack of* appearance and behavior indicating soundness and balance

- **un-R**obust: implies the *same* of all that are delicate or sickly

- **un-U**seful: *not* being of use or service, *not* serving some purpose, *not* producing material results

- **un-S**ound: emphasizes the *presence* of weakness, or malfunction

- **un- H**ale: applies particularly to *frailness* in old age, *not* strong, *not* well-conditioned

How is it that we sometimes form relationships that are so detrimental to us? To answer this question, it is important to acknowledge that they do not form accidentally, but rather intentionally, often on a subconscious level. As creatures of ritual and habit, we find comfort in what we are familiar with. This means that the relationships that we form (healthy or unhealthy) are often ones that we have once experienced and been *taught* from our family of origin to manage, rather than the relationships that benefit and enhance us as positive members of society. We need to be intentional and unrelenting in our pursuit of WRUSHing Relationships, in spite of an improper definition of "appropriate relationship" or what we are familiar with. Our purpose says that we are worth the extra mile to invest the energy into learning or forming WRUSHing Relationships with people that will support love, depend on and of us. As in waiting for anything that is good, the acquisitions of WRUSHing Relationships require our patience, devotion, and faith that what is good exists and that it is in our reach. Be patient, be devoted, and have faith that your divine purpose exists and that it is in your reach. Get equipped. Gather your troops and go for it!

THE PROFESSIONAL WOMAN NETWORK
Training and Certification on Women's Issues

Linda Ellis Eastman, President & CEO of The Professional Woman Network, has trained and certified over two thousand individuals to start their own consulting/seminar business. Women from such countries as Brazil, Argentina, the Bahamas, Costa Rica, Bermuda, Nigeria, South Africa, Malaysia, and Mexico have attended trainings.

Topics for certification include:
- Diversity & Multiculturalism
- Women's Issues
- Women: A Journey to Wellness
- Save Our Youth
- Teen Image & Social Etiquette
- Leadership & Empowerment Skills for Youth
- Customer Service & Professionalism
- Marketing a Consulting Practice
- Professional Coaching
- Professional Presentation Skills

If you are interested in learning more about becoming certified or about starting your own consulting/seminar business contact:

The Professional Woman Network
P.O. Box 333
Prospect, KY 40059
(502) 566-9900
lindaeastman@prodigy.net
www.prowoman.net

Youth Empowerment Series
Raising Healthy Children in an Unhealthy World

Women's Empowerment Series
Learning to Love Yourself: Self-Esteem for Women
A Journey Within: Self-Discovery for Women
The Woman's Handbook for Self-Confidence
Remove the Mask! Living an Authentic Life
The Woman's Handbook for Self-Empowerment
Becoming Your Own Best Friend
The Self-Architect: Redesigning Your Life

The African American Library
Learning to Love Yourself: A Handbook for the African American Woman
Wellness for the African American Woman: Mind, Body & Spririt
Life Skills for the African American Woman
Raising African American Boys
Raising African American Girls
Living Your Vision and Purpose
Bruised but not Broken

The Professional Woman Network - Book Series
Becoming the Professional Woman
Customer Service & Professionalism for Women
Self-Esteem & Empowerment for Women
The Young Woman's Guide for Personal Success

The Christian Woman's Guide for Personal Success
Survival Skills for the African-American Woman
Overcoming the SuperWoman Syndrome
You're on Stage! Image, Etiquette, Branding & Style
Women's Journey to Wellness: Mind, Body & Spirit
A Woman's Survival Guide for Obstacles, Transition & Change
Women as Leaders: Strategies for Empowerment & Communication
Beyond the Body! Developing Inner Beauty
The Young Man's Guide for Personal Success
Emotional Wellness for Women Volume I
Emotional Wellness for Women Volume II
Emotional Wellness for Women Volume III
The Baby Boomer's Handbook for Women

These books are available from the individual contributors, the publisher (www.pwnbooks.com), www.amazon.com, and your local bookstore by request.